To —

PAT — WITH FOND
MEMORIES OF CHRISTMAS
AT GRANTON-ON-SPEY
— 2013 —

(KEEP ON WATCHING
THE SCENERY AND
DONT LISTEN TO
ACCORDIANS) ! ! !

REGARDS.

MARY AND ROY.

XX

(THANK YOU FOR THE CHOCOLATES)

now we are
PAST IT

now we are
PAST IT

by **ALLISON VALE**

Michael O'Mara Books Limited

First published in Great Britain in 2011 by
Michael O'Mara Books Limited
9 Lion Yard
Tremadoc Road
London SW4 7NQ

A CIP catalogue record for this book is available from the British
Library.

Papers used by Michael O'Mara Books Limited are natural,
recyclable products made from wood grown in sustainable forests.
The manufacturing processes conform to the environmental
regulations of the country of origin.

ISBN: 978-1-84317-579-7

1 2 3 4 5 6 7 8 9 10

Cover design by Mint Julep
Cover photograph by Roger Dixon
Back cover photograph by Shutterstock
Illustrations by Andrew Pinder
Text design and typesetting by K DESIGN, Winscombe, Somerset

Printed and bound in Great Britain by Clays Ltd, St Ives plc

www.mombooks.com

For Mike,

Because if we're not already past it,

I reckon we're not far off . . .

With love,

AV

Contents

Introduction

Anyone who's recently passed a milestone birthday and immediately fled, panic-stricken, to the nearest Bikram yoga centre, knows the horror that sets in when you first realize you are Middle-Aged. For a while, you kid yourself that the advance of time is nothing; your iTunes account, salsa lessons and that glorious set of reflective Lycra cycling gear stand proudly blocking its path. You're only as old as you feel, and you feel great.

Great, that is, until the day your son or daughter sneers at your playlist, gags at the sight of you and your partner gyrating to Radio 1 in the kitchen or leaves you for dust when you're out for a jog. Bleakly, you realize you can't fool yourself forever: face it, a nice set of carpet slippers are starting to seem an alluring indoor footwear option and you can't think why you haven't always used a coaster under your drink. You can't even drown your sorrows like you used to: it takes you three days to get over the hangover. Whichever way you swing it, middle age has arrived.

The first thing to do is to get the midlife crisis over with. Go ahead and get your navel pierced, tattoo that flabby bicep, renew your gym membership or make a move on the office hottie. Whatever floats your boat – just get over it. And then, when you're left wondering what all the fuss was about, take a little time to decide what happens next. How is the rest of your life going to pan out? What are the options? Are you going to get yourself the best shed on the block and cultivate a passion for home-grown broccoli? Work on your golf handicap, take up membership of a wine club and look forward to an annual cruise?

Or is this all too soon? Well, the good news is that it doesn't have to be that way. These days, middle age brings with it freedoms worth celebrating. You've got the clarity to know what you want and the experience to know how to get it. Gone are the days of gorging on a late-night kebab in the pouring rain, while standing in line for the night bus home. No longer will you be expected to look ripped in your trunks or buff in your bikini, pitch a tent at a rock festival or devote all your free time to maintaining your *Call of Duty* kill rate.

Comfort-wear is where it's at and you can finally admit to yourself that rock festivals always made you tired and irritable. And dirty.

It's time to embrace your age-related wisdom; what's more, now you get to lord it up over the younger generation. Who cares if you're irritating, embarrassing or a bore? You've earned the right to tell it like it is and you no longer need to settle for anything less than precisely what you want.

And, hey, if it all goes wrong, you can always blame it on 'the youth of today'. What have you got to lose?

Time for Reinvention

Have you reached the life stage where your own 'adulthood' is no longer deniable? That 'Certain Age' when suddenly everyone you know has become rather staid and conventional? Do sober dinner parties and smug barbecues on decked terraces threaten to clog up your weekends? Is the conversation around you a relentless cycle of Sancerre and house prices? Are you beginning to wonder whether there is, in fact, life beyond middle age?

If so, it's high time you rebel, and not just by dressing for dinner in ripped jeans and battered Doc Martens.

Too Old to Party?

Sooner or later we all have to face up to the fact that the days of partying till dawn and still making it into work the next morning are over. These days, a night on the sauce on a Saturday can leave you still feeling jaded on

Monday morning. It's time to learn to pace yourself. Know your own limits. Comedian Micky Flanagan, a Londoner fast approaching middle age, admitted recently, 'I can't do this partying any more . . . I've reached the point where if I queue for a nightclub and the bouncer says, "You can come in," I say, "Thanks, mate . . . my feet are killing me."'

'I hate middle age. Too young for the bowling green, too old for Ecstasy.'

GREGOR FISHER, IN SITCOM *RAB C. NESBITT*

Are You Old Before Your Time?

Perhaps it's time to take stock. Just how close are you to premature maturity? Take a deep breath and let this cautionary checklist help you to figure out whether you are old before your time.

◎ Waitresses have started to call you 'sweetie'

◎ You find yourself caring that the neighbour's kids play on your lawn

◎ You care about your lawn

◎ Saturday nights are less about clubbing and more about *Strictly Come Dancing*

◎ You get twitchy when anyone puts their coffee mug down on the table without a coaster

◎ You own a set of coasters

- ◎ You own a set of fine bone china mugs you bought to match the coasters

- ◎ At hospital appointments, when an apparently pubescent medic starts examining you, you wonder aloud where the 'real' doctor is

- ◎ You turn down the offer of a night out on the basis that you've been out once already this weekend

- ◎ You wake with that 'morning after' feeling and all you did was to stay up to paint the living room. Until the news came on

- ◎ All your luggage is on wheels

- ◎ You make that spontaneous 'old man noise' every time you get out of a chair

- ◎ Your wardrobe's so outdated it's almost vintage

'I've always been older than I am. I was a middle-aged adolescent in tweed trousers.'

DANIEL KITSON, COMEDIAN

'I can feel myself getting older. The problem is, it creeps up on you like a Ninja. You think to yourself, "Ooh, I'm really young," then one day you catch yourself tucking your shirt into your underpants.'

JEFF GREEN, COMEDIAN

Finding Middle-Age Cool

Reinventing yourself can be as simple as discovering an all-new middle-aged cool. There are plenty of role models out there, so for inspiration you need do nothing more than keep your eyes peeled. As US comedian Demitri Martin discovered, a little observation can go a long way when it comes to figuring out a working definition of 'cool': 'I was at a party the other night, and I saw a guy wearing a leather jacket, and I thought, "That is cool." Like, ten minutes later, I saw a guy wearing a leather vest and I thought, "That is not cool." That's when I realized cool is all about leather *sleeves*.'

'One of the delights known to age, and beyond the grasp of youth, is that of Not Going.'

J.B. PRIESTLEY, PLAYWRIGHT

The Rock-Bottom Remainders

By the time you've hit true maturity, if all's gone according to plan, you should be enjoying some prowess at your chosen trade. You've worked long and hard to hone your skills and you've built a solid reputation in the process. Of course, there will always be those who reach the top rung only to discover they've been climbing the wrong ladder all along. These are the types who harbour a deep-seated hankering for something entirely different, which no amount of success can quash.

Take, for instance some of most successful living writers; Amy Tan, Steven King, Matt Groening, Ridley Pearson and Dave Barry. Their work is recognized the world over and has ensured that they can look forward to living out their days in comfort. But they discovered they had common ground beyond their ability to write: none of them had ever shaken off a desire to be in a rock band. It didn't take long for 'The Rock-Bottom Remainders' to be born.

The self-professed 'really bad' rock musicians were soon hailed by critics as having 'one of the world's highest ratios of noise to talent'. No surprise, given that they pay little attention to rehearsal or planning and a great deal more to general high-jinks and where to go for their slap-up post-gig dinner. They decided that at their stage in life, all that matters is having fun on their own terms.

They are also entirely sanguine about their small and idiosyncratic band of loyal followers. 'What I have found,' said Dave Barry, 'is that our groupies are ageing librarians and, even at my advanced age, I can outrun them pretty easily.'

'You've turned into your dad the day you put aside a thin piece of wood specifically to stir paint with.'

PETER KAY, COMEDIAN

Live the Dream. Period.

Middle-aged single, childless graphic artist Harry Finley lived what he described as 'a pretty dull life' in a small town in Maryland. But an interest that was first sparked when he lived and worked in Europe during the 1980s, took on a life of its own when Finley decided to turn his 'hobby' into a museum. His collection, the only one of its kind, attracted international press attention.

So – what is Finley's passion? Not what you might first imagine of a single male graphic artist. Finley is curator of the world's only Museum of Menstruation, an extensive collection of feminine hygiene products and vintage tampon advertisements from all over the world.

Finley is living proof that so long as you have the courage to stem the flow of an otherwise average existence, it's never too late to pursue your dream.

> 'If you are doing things the same as two years ago, you are almost certainly doing them wrong.'
>
> JOHN HARVEY-JONES, BUSINESSMAN

From One Circus Act to Another

A major life change is never easy; it takes a lot of courage to admit you're not happy – and more to do something about it. How much harder, then, when you have a face full of ink and are a professional freak-show act at Coney Island, lying on a bed of nails for a living under the name of 'The Pain-Proof Man'. That's exactly where Eduardo Arrocha had been for more than a decade. Bored of the daily grind, he yearned for mental stimulation, and finally made the decision, at forty-five, to go back to school to study law and take bar exams.

A model student, Eduardo soon made himself popular with his professors and with fellow undergraduates, and his former career came in handy during university vacations, when Eduardo the Geek would become Freak once more, eating light bulbs, walking on glass and clamping his tongue in a mousetrap for a little extra cash to pay for his textbooks.

As much as he loves his new career, he admits he finds the law more bizarre than any freak show.

'My career is going better now than when I was younger. It used to be that I'd get the girl but not the part. Now I get the part but not the girl.'

MICHAEL CAINE, ACTOR

Famous Failures

If you still need a little convincing that taking a risk
or two in middle adulthood might be worth a try, take
inspiration from some of the world's most famous
one-time 'failures'.

◎ Michael Jordan, widely hailed as one of the greatest
basketball players in the world, was cut from his
Varsity Basketball Team as a tenth grader because
he failed to stand out.

◎ Walt Disney's first cartoon company, 'Newman's
Laugh-O-Grams' made a spectacular loss and wound
up in bankruptcy proceedings.

◎ John Grisham, already a practising lawyer, tried
twenty-eight publishers before he persuaded one
small, barely known publishing house to take on his
first novel, *A Time To Kill*. His second novel, *The
Firm*, was a *New York Times* bestseller.

◎ Marilyn Monroe failed to impress Twentieth
Century Fox very early in her career, who refused
to renew her contract, finding her talentless and
unattractive.

'Anything that is worth doing has been done frequently. Things hitherto undone should be given, I suspect, a wide berth.'

MAX BEERBOHM, CARICATURIST

Fail Better

By the onset of middle age, it's all too easy to get comfortable with the way life has panned out, regardless of whether or not it's actually making you happy. Fear of failure is generally the biggest obstacle to change, leaving us reluctant to take a risk. But a little risk-taking can be a force for good. Like the great Irish playwright Samuel Beckett once said, 'Ever tried. Ever failed. No matter. Try Again. Fail again. Fail better.'

Quentin Crisp was a man who knew all too well the risks involved with being true to who you are. A flamboyant Englishman, who at various points in his life had been a prostitute, a journalist, a writer and raconteur and an actor, Crisp defiantly refused to hide his sexuality at a time when British society was institutionally homophobic. He once said, 'It's no good

22

running a pig farm badly for thirty years while saying, "Really I was meant to be a ballet dancer." By then, pigs will be your style.' It's advice worth taking.

'If you know you are going to fail, then fail gloriously!'

CATE BLANCHETT, ACTRESS

Dubya

If the world needs a better example of how the youthful fallen might still have a chance at becoming middle-aged and mighty, look no further than George W. Bush. As a young man, he had had a spectacular run of failed oil businesses under his belt, four in all, before turning to politics. Perhaps these early business failures inspired his razor-sharp observation that 'If we don't succeed, we run the risk of failure.' As US comedian Lewis Black commented, 'He's a man who was a failure until he was forty years old, which looks really good on your resume – if you're a comic.'

'In real life it is the hare who wins. Every time. Look around you. And in any case it is my contention that Aesop was writing for the tortoise market. Hares have no time to read. They are too busy winning the game.'

ANITA BROOKNER, NOVELIST

Middle-Aged Geek Chic

There's a degree of kudos these days to being a nerd. 'Geek chic' has been perpetuated by TV sitcoms such as *The Big Bang Theory* and *Glee*. It's now cool to be uncool – but don't be fooled, it's a rule that only works below a certain age. The closer you get to middle age, the more you tread perilous ground if you admit to a working understanding of binary maths or an ability to swear in Klingon.

Some of you may already be entirely settled in the world of the geek – way too comfortable with your leather elbow-patch sweaters and your box set of *Battlestar Galactica*. For the rest of you, there may still be some hope.

> 'Be nice to nerds. Chances are you'll end up working for one.'
>
> BILL GATES, BILLIONAIRE BUSINESSMAN AND PHILANTHROPIST

How geeky are you?

◎ Are you more interested in a movie's special effects than its plot lines?

◎ Do you, nevertheless, still memorize whole sections of movie dialogue the same way you used to when you were twelve?

◎ Do you own a rack of T-shirts with obscure slogans, such as, 'Alcohol & calculus don't mix. Never drink & derive', or 'Some things man was never meant to know. For everything else, there's Google'?

◎ Do you cling to your iPhone during an argument because you never know when you may need ready access to the net to prove that Roddenberry named Lieutenant Geordi La Forge (the one with the bionic spectacles from *Star Trek: Next Generation*) after his favourite Trekki.

◎ Do you suffer RAM envy?

◎ Have you named a child Leia, Luke, Kirk or Leonard?

◎ Who said: 'I know kung fu'?*

Geek or Nerd?

The youth lexicon seems to mutate every couple of months, and keeping up with it can be daunting. Take, for instance, those who are, shall we say, stylishly challenged: are the terms 'geek' and 'nerd' interchangeable, or do they apply to entirely different categories? American comedian Jacob Sirof thinks he has the answer, and is comfortable to label himself a geek, although he adamantly refuses to accept that he's a nerd.

'A geek is the kind of person that'll stand in line to see the midnight premiere of the new Harry Potter movie. That's me, that's how I roll . . .', he explains. 'Now a nerd is the kind of person who goes to the midnight premiere of the new Harry Potter movie dressed like Harry Potter. And that shit is pathetic, right? What's up with those losers?'

Thanks for clearing that up, Jacob.

---

* Neo, in *The Matrix*

Tron and *The Wizard Of Oz* were formative for me, so being able to be a part of things like *Tron*, *Twilight* and *Underworld*, it's much closer to where my heart lies. I'm a nerdy geek.'

MICHAEL SHEEN, ACTOR

The Dork Side

If you think you're too entrenched in your geeky ways to do anything about it, allow yourself to be inspired by a punk rock legend. Bryan 'Dexter' Holland, of American rock band The Offspring, has been hailed as 'one of the greatest punk vocalists in rock history' (according to the website IMDb), as well as being credited with bringing punk to middle-class, suburban America. But the wild man of American punk wasn't ever particularly feral. 'Dexter' was valedictorian of his high school in a wealthy Californian suburb and has a masters degree in molecular biology. If he can make the leap, so can you.

'I think I've been able to fool a lot of people because I know I'm a dork. I'm a geek.'

GWEN STEFANI, POP STAR

All Work and No Play

We've all come across the career maniac and, let's be honest, there's nothing worse. This is the individual who has lived to work for a couple of decades or more, and now has very little else. The kind of person who generally has no patience to sit through a movie and no inclination to eat in company; in any case, leisure time for them is such a rare thing, they have almost certainly forgotten how to fill it. Their Blackberry ranks as their most prized possession and life has become one endless cycle of work, gym and sleep.

If this all sounds horribly familiar, perhaps it's time you did something about it. Walk away from the mobile, take the whole weekend off and try really relaxing for once.

'Four years ago to this very date, I decided to take my own life. And I said, "Zach, do it in front of your co-workers and your manager at work. End the misery." I don't know how many of you have tried to jump off a Pizza Hut, but you really just get a sprained ankle out of the deal. And then you have to go back inside and serve Crazy Bread.'

ZACH GALIFIANAKIS, COMEDIAN

You Can't Take It With You

It's a good thing to be proud of your work. A dying trait, some might argue. But thinking up bizarre ways to take your work with you to the grave is perhaps a sign that your work-home balance needs a little readjustment.

◎ *Once You Pop* . . . In 1970 an organic chemist and food storage technician from Cincinnati named Frederic Bauer, designed and patented the iconic Pringles tube container. When he died in 2008 at the age of eighty-four, his family honoured his last wish: they buried his ashes in a Pringles can.

◎ *Immortalized in Print* . . . Comic book writer, editor and genius Mark Gruenwald, of Marvel Comics, died suddenly of a heart attack in 1996, at the age of just forty-two. Known in life as a practical joker, his final request involved family and colleagues in a uniquely bizarre act. Gruenwald's wish was granted: his cremated remains were mixed in with the ink for a print run of the trade collection of Mark's finest work, Squadron Supreme.

◎ *The Final Frontier . . .* Gene Roddenberry, the creator of the *Star Trek* TV series, wanted nothing more than for his ashes to be sent into space. When

They decided against cremation.

he died in 1997, his remains were taken up by a Spanish satellite and shot into the atmosphere to orbit the planet for eternity.

Every Urban Legend Has Its Moral

In 2001, a story about an employee of a New York publishing house went viral on the Internet. A Mr George Turklebaum had worked as a proofreader for the same company for three decades. He was a model employee: hard-working, thorough and compliant, he was always the first at his desk every morning and the last to leave at night.

So when a cleaner found him dead at his desk in the open-plan offices one Saturday morning, and the coroner established he had been dead since Monday, his bosses and co-workers were mortified that no one had noticed. It was a great story, picked up by the world press and even making its way into the BBC news, widely cited as having originated in the *The New York Times*. Such was the impact of the story that it made very little difference when it was eventually uncovered as nothing more than urban myth: the moral remained as powerful as any Aesop might have made. Never take your co-workers for granted: always give them a poke, just to be sure.

Although the ill-fated Mr George Turklebaum may never have existed beyond the realms of legend, his story is not without real-life precedent. In 2004, a 61-year-old employee of the Helsinki Tax Office died at his desk while working on tax returns. He wasn't discovered by any of the hundred or so colleagues working on the same floor for two whole days. Just goes to show that there's no point killing yourself working; nobody's going to notice.

'You can either see it as selfless dedication to public service broadcasting, or a shocking lack of ambition.'

JOHN PEEL, ON BEING A RADIO BROADCASTER
FOR MORE THAN FOUR DECADES

A Bum Deal

We can all suffer from an inflated sense of our own importance from time to time, particularly at work. But one high school art teacher from Virginia discovered that sometimes, a concerted effort not to take yourself too seriously can really pay off. Stephen Murmer from

Chesterfield, Virginia enjoyed sharing a unique form of self-expression on the US TV show *Unscrewed with Martin Sargent*. Disguised with a false nose, a towelling turban and a thong, he demonstrated the art of 'Butt Painting', smearing his buttocks and genitals with paint and imprinting them on canvas. When the clip hit YouTube, Murmer was quickly disciplined and sacked. However his lawyers, who referred to the school board's decision as 'a bad day for the First Amendment', took the case to court, whereupon Murmer was awarded compensation of more than $65,000. And of course, after all that publicity, his art works sold for an asstonishing $2,000 a piece.

Time for that Midlife Crisis

If you're just either side of forty, statistically you are more likely to be in the throes of a midlife crisis now than at any other time. That's according to a British study carried out in 2010. The decade beginning in your mid-thirties is loaded with stress. If you're not careful, long working hours, economic pressures, family responsibilities and the mounting physical signs of middle age conspire to send you into an emotional tailspin. But if you've escaped unscathed so far, perhaps now is the ideal time to start preparing yourself. The midlife crisis may have been worked to death by comedians and sitcom scriptwriters, but once you have one of your own, you'll know it's no joke.

'Here comes forty. I'm feeling my age and I've ordered the Ferrari. I'm going to get the whole midlife crisis package.'

KEANU REEVES, ACTOR

You're Ready for a Midlife Crisis If . . .

◎ You can name pretty much every member of the current cabinet

◎ You can only give your age these days if you do a quick mental calculation

◎ You have no trouble unfolding a broadsheet newspaper in a cramped space

◎ You always carry tissues and an umbrella, just in case

◎ You've finally started flossing

◎ These days a night out with your mates rarely involves more than a couple or three rounds, never ends in a curry and generally sees you home in time for the *Ten O'Clock News*

- ◎ Fashion looks suspiciously like those photos you have of your uni days

- ◎ You're frequently incensed by the poor grammar of waiters and shop assistants

- ◎ You regularly get your kids' names confused

- ◎ Your bathroom cabinet used to be stocked with a year's supply of condoms and Alka-Seltzer. These days, it's where you keep the cod liver oil capsules.

Keeping It Brief

US comedian Steve Cody is a self-titled 'midlife crisis comic'. He has all the classic signs of midlife crisis: silvering hair, a vigorous interest in mountain climbing and marathon running, and a shiny BMW M3. And, as he likes to share with his audiences, he has a growing intolerance of the over-use of small talk; an overwhelming impatience for those who are incapable of answering the question, 'How's it going?' with a single word, 'Fine.' Like his friend, Greg, for example. 'Greg never says fine', complained Steve. 'Instead I get, "Oh, Steve. I just got back from the doctor. My HDL level's too high, my LDL level's too low. Wait till you hear about my colonoscopy report." I know so much about Greg.'

'I'm secretly hoping it's a midlife crisis, meaning you're halfway to an early death.'

SUE (PLAYED BY JANE LYNCH) IN THE HIT TV SHOW *GLEE*

Mortality

Damon Wayans is a highly successful writer and *New York Times* best-selling novelist with no apparent cause for feeling the age-related blues. But as he explained, midlife crises can have very little to do with where you're at with your career and a whole lot to do with realizing you have very little time left to worry about getting old.

'A midlife crisis is the day that a man looks in the mirror and realizes he's no longer invincible. You see death in the reflection. That Grim Reaper looking at you going, "I got you in twenty years." And you try to fight it. You try to work out, but you start seeing that your chest turns into breasts.'

'Young guys go chasing women every night. You do that, you're called party animals. Do that in middle age, you're called a lonely alcoholic.'

MARK CRAIG TAYLOR, COMEDIAN

Once a Jerk, Always a Jerk

The past can be a difficult country, darkened by the uncomfortable realization that back then, when you thought you were witty, cool and on-trend, you were actually a pain in the ass. The trouble is, having identified this self-delusion of youth, midlife can bring with it the uncomfortable possibility that nothing has changed.

US comedian Jack Coen was struck by precisely this fear. 'I don't want to be younger, I really don't. Every time I look back a couple of years, I think, "God, what a jerk I was." But with that knowledge comes the realization that I'm a jerk right now. I think that's why old people get real quiet. They're like, "Man, I'm an idiot. I'm going to just stand right here."'

What's Your Poison?

Even for bright young things in their twenties, there's nothing like a hangover to give you a taste of what it's like to be 107 years old. And yet few of us ever entirely free ourselves from the lure of our favourite vice – whether that's a cold beer, a cool Chardonnay, a fresh pack of cigarettes or simply hot, strong coffee in plentiful supply. Oh yeah, we make empty pledges periodically, promising ourselves we'll either cut back or cut out but, as Humphrey Bogart once said, 'I gave up drinking once – it was the worst afternoon of my entire life.'

However, it's not all bad news. Latest studies confirm that not only is red wine a useful tool in the fight against heart disease, but it also has a positive effect at slowing the ageing of the eyes, as well as helping stave off cataracts. Of course, that nasty word 'moderation' cannot be overlooked, but pour yourself a restrained glass or two, and settle back to enjoy these tales of the overindulgence of others.

Blind Drunk

'One drink is just right; two is too many; three are too few.' So warns a Danish drinking proverb, as well it might to a nation with the most ready access to alcohol of any Scandinavian country. Danish-born writer and broadcaster Sandi Toksvig is well known for her intoxicating ability to spin a colourful yarn or two. She recently revealed on an episode of the television quiz show *QI* that her Danish grandfather happily shared the national predilection for a tipple. At some point in his life he had lost an eye.

'But he wasn't careless,' Sandi explained, 'he was ill.' He had had the eye replaced with an ice-blue glass eye, a perfect match to his good Scandinavian-blue one. But he didn't stop at just the one glass eye. 'He had [another] one made that was bloodshot. It was known

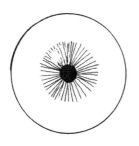 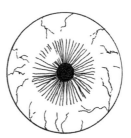

as, "Grandpa's Party Eye" and he kept it in a box on the mantelpiece. And when he was going out, he would take out the false blue one and put in the bloodshot one. He'd say, "I'm going out now and I shan't be back till they match!"'

> 'Sometimes getting older feels easy; sometimes it feels difficult. It depends how the wine is hitting you really.'
>
> RUPERT EVERETT, ACTOR

The Luck of the Irish?

'May you have the hindsight to know where you've been, the foresight to know where you're going and the insight to know when you're gone too far.' If the Irish need hard evidence of the sense in this old proverb, they only have to look to that huge star of stage and screen, native of Connemara, Peter O'Toole. A renowned party man, O'Toole recalled with satisfaction 'the days when one went for a beer at one's local bar in Paris and woke up in Corsica'. But more than a couple of decades of raising nightly hell took their toll on a 43-year-old Peter when he was rushed into hospital for emergency surgery on his abdomen. Peter stared death in the face when surgeons discovered that his digestive system had been ravaged by alcohol abuse.

After such a lucky escape, O'Toole had the insight to know that he had been going way too far and that his time for getting away with it was over. 'The time has come to stop roaming,' he said. 'The pirate ship has berthed. I can still make whoopee, but now I do it sober.' More than three decades on, this sagacity has ensured his longevity.

'As a hardened drinker, I don't need cures.'

TERRY WOGAN, TV PRESENTER

Drink Till You're Seeing Stars

No matter how old they get, some guys will still go to any lengths for a free pint. From statesmen to barmen, rocket scientists to motor mechanics, some guys never

turn down a beer. In 1995 *The New York Times* reported
the findings of Dr Tom Millar, a silver-haired
astrophysicist from the University of Manchester.
Dr Millar was one of a team of British scientists who
succeeded in analysing an interstellar gas cloud a
thousand times bigger than our solar system, and
discovered that it contains enough alcohol to make an
eye-watering 400 trillion trillion pints of beer. So
perhaps from now on astrophysicists will never die,
they'll head straight to that great *bierkeller* in the sky.

'I stopped drinking the day I couldn't find my way out
of a telephone box. I rang my manager in a panic. He told
me it couldn't be difficult. "There's only four walls and
the phone is on one of them for Christ's sake."'

BILLY CONNOLLY, COMEDIAN

Driving Under the Influence

When Dennis LeRoy Anderson, from Proctor, Minnesota, was arrested in August 2008 on a drink-driving charge outside his local bar, his blood alcohol level was more than three times over the legal limit. It was a common enough story: eight or nine beers, an ill-advised decision to drive home and the inevitable collision with another vehicle, in this case a stationary Dodge Intrepid parked outside the bar. And, as is so often the case, police on the scene also discovered that this wasn't Anderson's first drink-driving offence: he had, in fact, already had his licence revoked after a previous conviction.

But what made this incident all the more arresting was Anderson's 'vehicle'. Knowing he was legally prohibited from driving, he had come up with what he thought to be a viable alternative. He had fitted up his reclining armchair with a lawnmower motor and pimped it up with a steering wheel, headlights, a stereo, cup holders and a 'National Hot Rod Association' sticker on the headrest. That done, he had tootled along to his local bar in the comfort of his barker-lounger, travelling at a sedate 15 to 20 miles an hour.

Local police were surprised at the damage the motorized chair had been able to cause – both to the

driver and the parked-up Dodge – and Anderson received a suspended prison sentence and a hefty fine. The chair, meanwhile, was put up for auction. Deputy Police Chief Troy Foucault admitted to the local paper that he was highly tempted to put in a bid himself.

'My generation, faced as it grew with a choice between religious belief and existential despair, chose marijuana. Now we are in our Cabernet stage.'

PEGGY NOONAN, JOURNALIST AND WRITER

High on Life

It should come as no surprise that a large percentage of adults have dabbled in drugs at some point in their lives. Perhaps more surprising, though, is the revelation in the US press in January 2010 that the same generation is *still* dabbling. In fact, a substantial number of men and women have taken up smoking marijuana again in middle age, while many never really stopped. A recent study suggests that 5 million Americans over the age of fifty now admit to using drugs on a regular basis and that figure looks set to grow.

The words of American satirist Lenny Bruce now seem somewhat prophetic: 'Marijuana will be legal some day,' he predicted in the 1960s, 'because the many law students who now smoke pot will some day become congressmen and legalize it in order to protect themselves.'

'When I was in England, I experimented with marijuana a time or two, and I didn't like it and I didn't inhale and never tried it again.'

BILL CLINTON, FORMER US PRESIDENT

'I tried marijuana, didn't particularly like it and unlike President Clinton I did inhale.'

MO MOWLAM, BRITISH POLITICIAN

Remember When a Coffee Was Called a Coffee?

The new generation of coffee chain stores that have swept across the globe have a lot to answer for: coffee is no longer simply coffee. It's a statement, a fashion accessory; it is, in fact, part of a 'look'. So it might be refreshing to hear that it's not just the recently past-its who get frustrated with the nonsense that gets asked of coffee servers (forgive me, 'baristas'). Young US comedian Maria Bamford sees it as a sign of a generation with way too many civil liberties. She says it's often the moment you witness someone making an outrageously extravagant coffee order that you find yourself asking, 'Hey, maybe we have too much freedom in the United States?': 'Can I ask you a quick question about the coffee? Is it organic? OK, I don't want it, I don't want it. I'd like to have a bowl of boiling hot water – boiling, boiling – with ice, and I don't want the ice to get all tiny.'

'When I wake up in the morning, I just can't get started until I've had that first, piping hot pot of coffee. Oh, I've tried other enemas . . . '

EMO PHILIPS, COMEDIAN

Sex, drugs . . . and palm trees?

It sounds like a rock 'n' roll myth: a rock guitar legend living the high life in Fiji, with the help of close friends and just a sniff or two of cocaine. Sun, sea, sand and palm trees. Our rock star, feeling invincible after a night of narcotic indulgence, insists on shimmying up a huge palm tree. Seconds later, he plunges out of the tree and lands on his head. It's no myth: its just one of the many near-death experiences of Rolling Stone Keith Richards, who was clearly not so much invincible as, well, caned.

The fall was a nasty one, necessitating an emergency operation to fit a metal plate in his skull. But if you're imagining this to be a story from Richards's halcyon days in the 1960s, you'd be wrong. This was 2006, and the man, once dubbed 'The World's Most Elegantly Wasted Human Being', was sixty-three at the time. But, just to prove that it's never too late to turn over a new leaf, the Fiji incident proved to be the final jolt Richards needed. He hasn't taken cocaine since, and has been heroin-free for more than three decades. Perhaps there's hope for us all?

Body Trauma

Are you beginning to curse Newton and his God-awful theories every time you catch a glimpse of yourself naked? The uncomfortable truth is that as the ravaging effects of your days of sex, drugs and rock 'n' roll make themselves ever more apparent, you are fast approaching the most painful dilemma of the recently past it. How to proceed from here needs careful consideration.

Let's look at your options:

◎ Embrace the Church of Spanx, and invest in gravity-defying underwear that will prop up your sagging chest and strap down your flabby midriff

◎ Prostrate yourself under the surgeon's knife, allowing yourself to be sliced, pumped and re-modelled into better shape

◎ Worship at the altar of Madonna, embracing yoga and a raw food diet while adopting a brood of infants to keep you on your toes

If you are beginning to empathize with the late actor Richard Harris, who once said, 'My face is like five miles of bad country road', don't despair. Perhaps there's another way. Be true to who you are, vow to age disgracefully and throw a finger to the convention that only young is beautiful! As Billy Connolly says, 'Fuck handsome . . . rich works!'

'My husband said, "Show me your boobs," and I had to pull up my skirt . . . so it was time to get them done!'

DOLLY PARTON, COUNTRY SINGER

Letting It All Hang Out

Many of our more 'mature' celebrities show no urge to hide their bodies away and perhaps none more so than the indefatigable Bette Midler. Bette has been known to bare a boob or two mid-concert and she is candid about a peculiar preoccupation she has with her breasts: she likes to know how much they weigh. 'Got myself a little mail scale, the kind they weigh postage and cocaine on. Unhooked my bra, flopped one of those suckers down . . . I won't tell ya how much they weigh but it costs $87.50 to send 'em to Brazil . . . third class!'

> 'I'd like to change my butt. It hangs a little too long. God forbid what it will look like when I'm older. It will probably be dragging on the ground behind me.'
>
> TERI HATCHER, ACTRESS

The Seventh Deadly Sin

When Al Pacino confessed, 'Vanity is my favourite sin', he was probably giving voice to something many of us are guilty of. But, taken too far, vanity can get you into some pretty dodgy territory. Take, for example, the 46-year-old man so keen to get back his youthful appearance, he treated himself to a facelift for his birthday. All went well, and upon his release from the clinic he decided to pop into the corner store on his way home to trial-run his new look. He said to the shopkeeper, 'I've just had a birthday. Indulge me, how old would you say I am?'

The shopkeeper checked him out thoughtfully and answered, 'I would say you're not a day over thirty-two.'

'Awesome,' he replied. 'I'm actually forty-six. And you've made my day.'

Enjoying the flattery, the man decided to stop at the hot-dog stand, where he made his order and asked the vendor the same question. 'To me, you look around thirty,' was the answer. Again, he boasted his real age and walked away to the bus stop with a jaunty step.

Unable to resist one last try, the man put the same question to an old lady waiting for the bus.

'I'm seventy-eight years old and my eyes are not what they used to be,' she replied. 'But if you really wanna know, I used to be able to tell a guy's exact age by taking a look at what's hanging inside his shorts.'

The man weighed the offer up. On the one hand, exposing Big Dick and the Twins on the street wasn't his style. On the other, he was on a roll and curious. So in a flash, he whipped out his tackle and let the old girl check him out.

After a good long look, and with a glint in her eye, she finally announced, 'You're forty-six years old!'

'That's impressive' he said, zipping himself back up. 'How can you tell?'

'I was behind you at the hot-dog stand' the old girl replied.

'The thing you notice here after America is how refreshingly ordinary people look because they haven't had their chin wrapped around the back of their ears.'

SIR IAN MCKELLEN, ACTOR

An Indecorous Way to Go

Whenever you opt to go under the surgeon's knife, you're taking a huge leap of faith that they will act safely, ethically and as you have requested. We've all heard the horror stories about when cosmetic surgery goes horribly wrong. And every once in a while, a procedure turns out to be deadly.

Hugh Massingberd, a former editor of the obituaries page of *The Daily Telegraph*, recalled in an article for the *Spectator,* how he had once been instructed by the editor of *The Telegraph* to include a cause of death in every obit. Massingberd felt this to be an unseemly requirement, which he demonstrated the following day by running an obit for an American jazz player who had, as he put it, 'handed in his dinner pail after a penile implant had unfortunately exploded'. Having proved his point, the editor capitulated.

As for the jazz player: well, isn't that a story that will make you count your blessings (in inches)?

'The media would have us believe that ageing is harder for women, which might be true, but then, hey, men age too. For example, how hairy are my toes becoming?'

JEFF GREEN, COMEDIAN

An Entirely New Relationship with Breasts

Lots of men will identify with the trials and tribulations of middle-aged writer and journalist Stephen J. Lyons, who has been open about his ongoing battle with his ageing body. His altered experience of the locker-room will be familiar enough to most midlife men: gone are the days when you could gambol naked and proud, playing whiplash by snapping your towel. Writing on the website salon.com, he complains: 'Showers are not for lingering anymore, nor can I comfortably flex and strut in front of a mirror. Instead, when I sneak a peek at my reflection, I notice . . . a disturbing jiggling motion around the chest area. Breasts! When I bend over, cleavage! Although most men adore breasts, they do not want their own pair . . .'

'You go to the gym, right, and they got a machine for every body part. You know – they got something for the legs, the arms, the back. But you know, you can't walk up to the trainer and be like, "Where's the man-tit machine at?"'

TODD LYNN, COMEDIAN

Hugh's Brief Encounter

Let's face it, the physical discomforts of middle age can be unpleasant – and to add insult to injury, there's a whole new world of invasive medical check-ups waiting just around the corner. Billy Connolly sums it up nicely, 'See, there's a terrible thing happens to men after fifty: your doctor loses all interest in your testicles, and takes an overwhelming interest in your arsehole.'

Hugh Grant is no stranger to embarrassment; let's face it, he has a history of being discovered in compromising positions. But I digress. A few years ago, he was horrified to discover during a long train journey that he had been struck with one of the ugly secrets of middle age: haemorrhoids.

'I felt something strange in my buttocks. As I had never had haemorrhoids, I did not understand what was happening,' he confessed in a magazine interview. He decided to head to the toilet to investigate further. 'But it was damn hard, because it was a small toilet. I finished up standing on the bezel . . . [trying to bend and] twist myself to see myself in the mirror. But, like a fool, I forgot to lock the door. And when I had my buttocks wide open, a woman entered the toilet and found herself nose to nose with the most intimate part of my anatomy . . . '

'I don't need you to remind me of my age. I have a bladder to do that for me.'

STEPHEN FRY, TV PRESENTER AND ACTOR

> 'I feel very, very old. My hair hurts. I have buttocks all over my body and I can't even smoke properly any more. I don't have lungs; I just have two poppadoms in here.'
>
> DYLAN MORAN, COMEDIAN

Time to Dye?

It starts with the odd grey hair, quickly pulled out in horror, then it spreads across your temples and before you know it you're at the pharmacy asking for DIY hair dye labelled Autumn Chestnut. There's no question that greying hair is ageing. But less commonly discussed is whether there is a need to colour greying hair in less visible areas . . . In 2003, an episode of *Sex in the City* addressed this very issue when man-eater Samantha was horrified to discover a single grey pubic hair. Deciding to colour her way out of the situation, Sam then left the colour treatment on for too long, resulting in flaming red pubes.

> 'I'm getting to an age when I can only enjoy alphabetti spaghetti if I'm wearing my reading glasses.'
>
> FRANK SKINNER, COMEDIAN

> 'I found my first grey pubic hair the other day. It was in a kebab, but there you go.'
>
> JEFF GREEN, COMEDIAN

Sorry For Your Loss

A receding hairline in your late twenties can get you down. An expanding bald patch in your late thirties is depressing. By your forties, it's possible we're not talking 'hair' so much as, 'hairs'. The trouble is that just as you come to terms with your current state of hair loss, you can be sure that an all-new stage is waiting just around the corner. And coaxing you into parting with your hard-earned cash to combat your moulting is, of course, a multibillion dollar global industry. So in case

you're ever tempted to splash out on largely ineffectual, artificial anti-hair-loss treatments, pay an uplifting visit to baldrus.com, a website devoted to high-fiving the hairless, and urging men everywhere to 'just say no to rugs, drugs, plugs . . . and comb-overs'.

Men Care About Ageing Too

As we all know, the anti-ageing industry isn't just big bucks for a female market. As US comedian Greg Fitzsimmons says, male ageing is a big business too, just take a look at the big money-spinners in the pharmaceutical industry. 'These are the big breakthroughs in science and technology in the last ten years: we have Rogaine, Prozac, now we have Viagra. You get a sense for who's bankrolling medical research in this country. It's just depressed, balding, white guys who can't get erections anymore.'

'I'm getting a little older and starting to understand women a little better. I'm haven't gotten any smarter, it's just now when I jog, my tits hurt too.'

ERIK LUNDY, COMEDIAN

Sporting Injuries

A curious consequence of the ageing process is a subtle change in how you spend your free time. In your younger days, down time was all about long nights in the pub followed by drunken karoke. Weekend rock festivals, midweek comedy gigs and the odd house party was where it was at.

But soon enough, career, family and responsibility make an evil pact to ensure that you simply don't have the stamina for too much late-night fun. Weekends are set aside for an entirely new range of leisure pursuits, many of which are a reaction to the onset of Middle-Aged Spread. Open your wardrobe and there's a good chance there'll be Lycra lurking in there somewhere. Perhaps a racing bike, suspended from the garage wall. Or even (God forbid!) a set of golf clubs in the boot.

Plus Fours or Lycra?

These days, everyone has taken up cycling. It's all about showing off your rock-hard glutes in shiny Lycra. The press have dubbed them 'MAMILS': Middle-Aged Men in Lycra. Perhaps it's the lure of skintight shiny outfits, irresistible for the generation who just missed out on Spandex, and grew up on comic book heroes. Whatever the reason, statistics show that British men between the ages of thirty-five and forty-five now favour a state-of-the-art bicycle, where once they might have opted for a Porsche and golf club membership.

So where does this leave golf? Is being keen on the green still OK? Actor and comedian Robin Williams thinks not. He says that only a Scot with a wily sense of humour could have invented a game where the aim is to hit a tiny ball into a tiny hole, hundreds of yards away, hindered by sand banks, scrub and vast garden ponds. But plenty of midlifers continue to buy into what Williams calls that 'manly sport . . . where you can dress like a pimp and no one will care'.

'There's another warning sign of old age: golf. It's nature's way of telling you should be dead.'

ERIC IDLE, COMEDIAN, ACTOR AND WRITER

Anything but Exercise!

However much we might hate it, there comes a time when a guy has to man-up to the need to get in shape. The excess booze, the cigarettes and the fast-food diet have to go once you get to a certain age. And if you indulged in all those bad habits, it can be tough trying to tackle them all at once.

US comedian Gene Pompa knows exactly how tough. 'I quit smoking cigarettes about a year ago,' he told an audience recently. 'I gained eighteen pounds. So now I have to wear a lot of black so no one knows what a big hunk of pig I turned into. No matter what I do, I cannot lose this eighteen pounds. It's really starting to kick my ass. I mean I have tried everything short of diet and exercise.'

How to Lose the Love Handles

If you've gained a few pounds here and there over the years, stepping up the fitness regime should help you shift them. But if you've gained a few pounds *everywhere*, there's no avoiding it: you're going to have to diet. And choosing the right diet for you can be tricky.

US comedian J. Anthony Brown happened upon the perfect diet for him after reading an interview with the late great Barry White: 'He said what he did was take all of his clothes off, and he stood naked in front of the mirror. I said, "That's a damn good diet." I think I could lose weight, too, if I saw Barry White naked, huh? Like, "You hungry?" "No man, I just saw Barry White naked. I don't want nothing."'

The Devoted Husband

A Manchester United football fan was unhappy with his seat at Old Trafford. Scanning the stadium, he spotted a vacant seat on the midline. He picked his way down through the rows until he reached the empty seat, asking the guy sitting alongside it whether it was taken.

'No, mate. It was my wife's seat but she passed away. She never missed a game,' the guy replied, without taking his eyes off the pitch.

Expressing his sympathy, the Man U fan asked why the man had not brought someone else along to fill the seat.

'I would have done,' he replied. 'But they're all at the funeral.'

'Cigarettes, whisky and wild, wild women.'

HENRY ALLINGHAM, SUPERCENTENARION,
ON THE SECRET OF LONGEVITY

The Blind Leading the Ridiculous

Middle-aged Kevin has played golf religiously every Sunday for the last ten years. But Kevin's short-sightedness means that without his glasses, he is blind on the green. So when he wakes up one Sunday morning ready for a swift eighteen holes to discover he has stepped on his glasses in the night and broken them, he is devastated.

'I'll not be able to play till I get a new pair', he tells his wife, Ann, with heavy heart. Ann has come to love her quiet Sunday mornings and is not about to let a pair of broken glasses get in her way.

'Why don't you take your father with you?' She suggests. 'He has perfect vision since his laser surgery. He can spot the ball for you.'

So Kevin calls his dad and heads off for the golf club. At the first hole, Kevin lines himself up as best he can, and sends the ball sailing off into the distance.

'See it?' asks Kevin.

'Course I did. What a beauty!' remarks his father.

'Where'd it go?'

'I don't remember.'

> 'If the devil were to offer me a resurgence of what is commonly called virility, I'd decline. "Just keep my liver and lungs in good working order," I'd reply, "so I can go on drinking and smoking!"'
>
> LUIS BUÑUEL, FILM-MAKER

Marathon Man

So if you're going to adopt a fitness regime to stave off old age and decrepitude, you're going to do it properly, right? No half measures. For you it's all about endurance, staying the course, pitching yourself against, well . . . yourself. And emerging triumphant, right? What better than the marathon? It's all about you: no team spirit to keep you going. The ultimate test of your metal.

All well and good if you're up to the challenge, but what if it turns out you're not? US comedian David Alan

Grier discovered this to his cost. 'He blows that pistol off, and you're running. Oh, you're waving – "Look at me, I'm running a marathon!" Oh and it's great. It is exciting! It is exciting for about a mile-and-a-half.'

The Long Pursuit of the Perfect Gym Body

Some bodies are just not meant for muscle – and if you've not learned that by now, maybe its time you got real. Comedian Mike Birbiglia has learned the hard way.

'I try and go to the gym. But it seems kind of counterproductive because the idea is to impress women, but there are women at the gym and they can see me bench-pressing sixty-five pounds. And I don't think they're saying, "Check out the guy in the dress socks. I saw him do one chin-up and then fall on the ground."'

Tee for Two

A sailor is stranded on a desert island all alone after his ship goes down. Year after year, the man builds SOS fires and tries not to lose hope of a rescue. Finally one day, a beautiful woman strides out of the sea in full scuba gear. The sailor is overcome.

'How long has it been since you had a smoke?' she asks him.

'Five years,' he tells her. She unzips a pocket and pulls out a perfectly dry pack of cigarettes, lighting one up for him.

'Bliss,' he says, after a taking a long drag.

'And how long have you gone without beer?' she asks.

'The beer all went down with the ship too, five years ago' he says pitifully.

She unzips a waterproof bag strapped to her hips and pulls out an ice-cold six-pack. Cracking open a can, he can't believe his luck.

'Amazing,' he sighs.

Then she begins to slowly unzip the wetsuit.

'So I guess it's been five long years since you've had any real fun?'

At this, the man is hardly able to contain himself, and, tears welling up in his eyes, exclaims, 'Don't tell me you've a set of clubs in there too?'

'What do you do – eat the right foods, exercise? Live till you're ninety-seven so your relatives can empty your urine bottle every five minutes? Oh, thanks for living so long, Grandpa. All I want to do is tend to your bodily fluids!'

JOEY KOLA, COMEDIAN

> 'If you really want to get better at golf, go back and take it up at a much earlier age.'
>
> THOMAS MULLIGAN, GOLFER

Exactly How Active Is Active?

It's old news that we in the West are getting fatter and lazier. Mechanization, easy transport and sedentary lifestyles along with fast food and bad diets are dooming us to obesity. We know that already. We also know we need to take personal responsibility to sort ourselves and our children out. But periodically it falls on public and government sponsored agencies to try to establish quite how bad the situation is.

In 2003, America's Center for Disease Control and Prevention decided to take a survey into American lifestyles, the second such survey it had undertaken. This time, to get a more comprehensive picture of exactly how active the American nation was, the CDC decided to loosen its definition of 'activity'. Moderate exercise had been defined in earlier surveys: gardening, walking, housework, ballroom dancing and so on. This time, they decided to ask Americans about the extent of their indulgence in 'light activity', including fishing sitting down, shooting a pistol, photocopying, playing darts or pool, colouring-in, taking a whirlpool bath and even 'purposeless wandering'. Even with these generous allowances, the CDC concluded bleakly that Americans just aren't active enough.

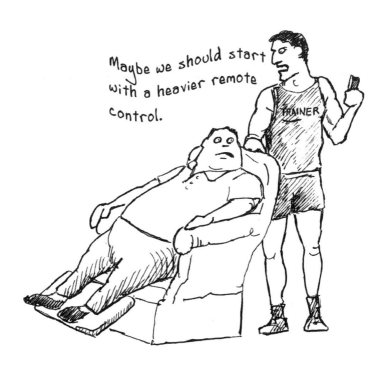

When a Golfer Loses His Drive

When your sport is your passion, your career *and* your relaxation, it can come to dominate your life. Which is fine, until the time comes when you feel too old for the game and you find yourself with a whole lot of time on your hands.

George Archer was a celebrated American golfer, who won the US Masters a total of nineteen times. In later life, contemplating retirement, he was faced with a tough conundrum. 'Baseball players quit playing and take up golf. Basketball players quit and take up golf. Football players quit and take up golf,' he would tell people when asked about his plans. 'What are we supposed to do when we quit?'

Team Player, But Lazy

For those of you who miss the camaraderie of your days on the team, but who just don't have the desire to get out of breath, why not check out the newly emerging sport of Segway polo? Segways turn a nifty corner with ease while removing any risk of a raised heart-rate; perfect for taking the effort out of the fast-paced game of polo. Created by Apple co-founder Steve Wozniak, the sport even has its own league, consisting of teams all competing for the Woz Challenge Cup, a tournament described in one American newspaper as dominated by 'the pudgy and the pale'. Perfect!

Telling It
Like It Is

Do you show no mercy when confronted with poor service? Do you impatiently correct ham-fisted answers on *The Weakest Link*? Are you goaded into noisy objection whenever you're subjected to all that 'global

warming' nonsense? And, be honest, how many times have you considered writing to the newspapers about yet another piece of nonsense on TV?

This may sound suspiciously like the onset of grumpy old age, but the chances are this is nothing new; maybe you're just as noisily resistant to convention as you've always been.

In fact, it's high time you celebrated your right to be stridently opinionated. So the next time anyone dares to tells you you're past it, don't be tempted to turn tactful! Stand up and tell it like it is.

'I wish people who have trouble communicating would just shut up.'

TOM LEHRER, SONGWRITER

Venomous Viv

Designer Vivienne Westwood, the cheerleader of mature miscreants everywhere, scorns all attempts at polite platitude in favour of an altogether more straight-talking approach. She recently swept into London's Ivy Club, where she spotted writer Stephanie Theobald,

whose most recent novel, *A Partial Indulgence*,
Vivienne had just read.

'I don't like your novels,' spat Vivienne, unprompted,
talons outstretched. 'And this one is like vomit coming
at you off the page, actually. I mean, I *really* hate your
writing.' As Theobald sat in stunned silence, Vivienne's
attentions moved on to actor Alex Jennings, who had
just appeared as the Prince of Wales in *The Queen*. 'That
was an absolutely terrible film,' she bellowed at him
across the room. Say what you mean, Viv!

> 'If life were fair, Dan Quayle would be asking, "Would you
> like fries with that?"'
>
> JOHN CLEESE, ACTOR

Time to Get Creative with the Truth

Age can bring with it a newfound confidence to speak
your mind and often this can be put to best effect when
it's used creatively. Take for example 51-year-old Italian
artist Maurizio Cattelan, known for his controversial
works of art. Recently commissioned to produce a

statue for the piazza in front of Milan's Stock Exchange, Cattelan didn't miss the opportunity to express exactly how he felt about the state of his country's finances. In fact, his finished work raised a finger to the financial quarter, quite literally: it was a 36-foot-high hand, the middle finger standing erect, positioned pointedly in front of the Stock Exchange. Journalists the world over couldn't fail to spot the message, leaving the artist himself with no need to express his viewpoint verbally.

'What's the point in growing old if you can't hound and persecute the young?'

KENNETH CLARKE, BRITISH POLITICIAN

Don't Hold Back, Doc

A city banker thought he'd visit his doctor for a thorough check-up. The consultant, a sharply dressed woman in her late forties, put him through a long barrage of tests before finally putting away her charts.

'Well, you're doing OK, all things considered,' she concluded casually.

Picking up on her distinct lack of enthusiasm about the state of his health, the banker asked with some trepidation, 'So how do you fancy my chances of living to be a hundred?'

'Do you smoke or drink?' she asked.

'No', he answered smugly. 'I quit ten years ago.'

'Eat much beef or fried foods?'

'Hardly at all. I work really hard to cut out cholesterol,' he assured her.

'Do you spend a lot of time in the sun, when you're holidaying abroad, playing golf, sailing or cycling?'

'No, I don't,' he said, his confidence growing. 'I try to keep out of direct sunlight and keep fit by spending an hour a day on my home treadmill.'

'So do you speed, gamble, take recreational drugs or have a lot of sexual partners?'

'No, none of those things,' he replied.

The doctor took a long hard look at him, making no attempt to disguise her disdain, before asking, 'In that case, why the hell would you want to carry on living?'

'I wouldn't say I was grumpy. It's more pathological –
I have seismic tantrums. I get red in the face and cry at
least three times a week, and I have to lie down and have
a nap afterwards . . . I'm in that late forties/early fifties
second toddlerhood phase.'

JENNY ECLAIR, WRITER AND COMEDIAN

You Cannot Be Serious?

John McEnroe is revered the world over as the
godfather of giving-it-to-them-straight. Mostly, his
verbal venom has been reserved for linesmen and
umpires; like the time he begged a British policeman to
arrest the 'incompetent old fool' of an umpire at
Wimbledon in 1981. Or the time he called an umpire at
the Stockholm Open a 'jerk'.

The crowds grew to love his schoolboy tantrums, but
only the bravest would risk heckling him. In 1992, one
fan made the mistake of persistently heckling McEnroe
at Key Biscayne in Florida. Finally, mid-serve, the
tennis player could take no more. Turning to the guy,
McEnroe asked, 'Do you have any problems, other than
that you're unemployed and a moron and a dork?'

Things It's Now OK to Hate

◎ Dancing in public

◎ Anyone who begins their order at a coffee bar with the phrase, 'Can I get . . . '

◎ People who use the term 'closure' in an attempt to sound emotionally in-tune

◎ Texting, tweeting and Face-ache

◎ Novelty ringtones

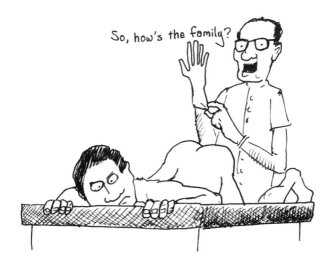

- ◎ Reality TV 'stars', talentless celebrities and anyone with a boob-job or hair implants

- ◎ Office 'Secret Santas'

- ◎ Team-building daytrips

- ◎ Men who wear kilts to weddings, even when they're not really Scottish

- ◎ Older guys than you who date younger women

- ◎ Younger women who date older men

- ◎ Discovering someone's put the cheese back into the fridge uncovered and now it's gone all crusty

- ◎ Doctors who make small-talk during intimate examinations

'Beware of the young doctor and the old barber.'

BENJAMIN FRANKLIN, STATESMAN AND FOUNDING FATHER

Word to the Wise

There may not be a whole lot of benefits to getting older, but, as the ultra-smooth French singer Maurice Chevalier once said, 'Old age isn't so bad when you consider the alternative', so maybe it's time to count your blessings.

One silver lining is a generous serving of extra wisdom. So perhaps it's time to stop grumbling about the 'youth of today' and instead embrace the wise old guru that lies deep within. It's time to start giving others the benefit of your advice.

'Then there's a friend who only calls me when she's depressed. You all know people like this: I'm on the phone with her for three hours; it's a waste of time. She never listens to my advice – she will not jump.'

CAROL SISKIND, COMEDIAN

Be Succinct

The sagest advice is often short and to the point. No one likes to have to sit and listen to a rambling monologue when all they really need is a straightforward answer to a simple question. But sometimes, that succinct advice is not necessarily entirely welcomed. While serving as the BBC's adviser on Roman Catholic affairs, Father Andrew Agnellus received a letter from a TV producer, asking how he should go about finding out about the Roman Catholic stance on heaven and hell. Father Agnellus offered him a one-word memo by way of reply: 'Die.'

What to Do When You're All Out of Advice

When you yearn to be a shining beacon of wisdom, but you're all out of good advice, the best plan is to borrow someone else's . . .

◎   'Be nice to people on your way up because you'll meet them on your way down.'
WILSON MIZNER, PLAYWRIGHT

◎   'If you can't convince them, confuse them.'
HARRY S. TRUMAN, FORMER US PRESIDENT

◎ 'Marriage is too interesting an experiment to be tried only once.'
EVA GABOR, ACTRESS

◎ 'Start every day off with a smile and get it over with.'
W. C. FIELDS, ACTOR AND WRITER

◎ 'I always advise people never to give advice.'
P. G. WODEHOUSE, NOVELIST

◎ 'If it has tyres or testicles, you're going to have trouble with it.'
LINDA FURNEY, FORMER OHIO SENATOR

◎ 'The future will be better tomorrow.'
DAN QUAYLE, ACTOR

◎ 'Never believe in mirrors or newspapers. '
TOM STOPPARD, PLAYWRIGHT

◎ 'Let me give you one word of advice: never go to a sex shop when you're horny. You have no idea what you're going to end up with – make a list; stick to the list.'
WENDY SPERO, COMIC

That's the MD. He likes rap music and practical jokes.

The Eternal Optimist

The best advice is always that which has an intrinsic note of optimism. Woodie Held, an amiable baseball player through the 1950s, was famed among sporting circles for his upbeat, off-kilter advice. 'Don't forget to swing hard,' he would tell hitters, 'in case you hit the ball.'

Dumb Advice

Seeking professional advice doesn't always guarantee quality: things aren't always better just because you've paid more for them. Sometimes a bit of homespun wisdom goes a lot further. American comic Robert Kelly discovered this for himself after seeking therapy for problems in the bedroom: 'I go to therapy now, too. He's such an ass. He really is. I told him I had problems keeping it up during sex, and his advice was to look my girl right in the eyes while we're having sex. That's great. How am I going to think of other chicks when I'm staring right at her?'

'A psychiatrist asks a lot of expensive questions your wife asks for nothing.'

JOEY ADAMS, COMEDIAN

Leave it to a Professional?

In another example of professional advice backfiring in style, in 1999, rap artist Dr Dre consulted a musicologist to ascertain whether he could legally incorporate a five-note bass-line from a 1980s hit called 'Backstrokin' into his new track. Assured by the professional go-ahead, Dr Dre was nonetheless sued for infringement of copyright to the tune of $1.5 million.

'Wisdom doesn't automatically come with old age. Nothing does — except wrinkles. It's true, some wines improve with age. But only if the grapes were good in the first place.'

ABIGAIL VAN BUREN, AGONY AUNT

A Word for the New Guy

It's always good to take the new person in the office into your confidence. Give them the low-down on office politics and welcome them into the fold with a few carefully chosen pieces of advice. It's an etiquette that goes all the way to the top. When Barack Obama was first elected to the Senate in 2004, Senator John McCain welcomed him by phone and passed on a valuable lesson. 'I told him Harry Truman said the truest thing. He said, "If you want a friend in Washington, get a dog."'

'Years ago we discovered the exact point the dead centre of middle age. It occurs when you are too young to take up golf and too old to rush up to the net.'

FRANKLIN PIERCE ADAMS, COLUMNIST

The Benefit of Experience

There's no time like the present to reflect on where you've come from, what you've learned along the way, and the knowledge you could easily have lived without.

◎ You were right at twelve years old: there really wouldn't be a time in adulthood when you'd need to use algebra

◎ The failures of others make the best dinner conversation

◎ All you really want from an obit is the cause of death

◎ There's a very fine line between boredom and hunger

◎ After forty, tiredness is pretty much a way of life

◎ There are days when you can ask someone to repeat a question two or three times and still have absolutely no idea what they just asked

◎ Caller ID is mankind's best invention: now you *know* who you're ignoring

◎ Practice really does make perfect. Proof? You can hit the snooze button with your eyes closed, every time

◎ Bad underwear can ruin your day

◎ Silences rarely need filling

◎ No matter how late at night you log onto Facebook, at least 25 per cent of your friends will still be awake

◎ There's a pretty good chance that you might never grow up

How Not To Be A Bore

It's a real fear of middle age, isn't it? That instead of imparting sage words of wisdom, we will begin to give voice to some of life's most excruciatingly dull thoughts. Dry rot and the price of sprouts have thus far been of little interest, but the terrifying thought that any day now, you might wake up with an involuntary need for this kind of conversational fodder can plague even the most vocally nimble of us.

'Called me dad to see if he had any news for me. "Nothing," he said. "Your mam has been out and bought a new toilet-brush holder, but the brush doesn't fit so she's just using it to put flowers in instead." They waste nothing, me mam and dad.'

FROM *KARLOLOGY – WHAT I'VE LEARNED SO FAR* BY KARL PILKINGTON

Man Bores Woman

It's the big question: is becoming an old bore a painful inevitability? *Daily Mail* columnist Liz Hodgkinson felt that it absolutely is. Well, for men, at least. 'When did most men in my age group become so stupefyingly dull?' Liz wanted to know. 'I can foresee a time when there will be swathes of ditched older men living alone with only the crossword for company, while women of the same age are having the time of their lives. Gentlemen, you have been warned. It's time to smarten up your act or face a lonely old age.'

Not surprisingly, her warning didn't go unchallenged. Old codgers everywhere had something to say in their defence, but Michael Bywater of *The Independent* had the last word: 'We know things. We aren't obsessed with ourselves. We've realized we're no oil painting. We cook like gods. We know where to take you, and how to get in. We think *Grand Theft Auto* is for losers and abs are for narcissists and girls under twenty-two. We notice your ideas as well as your underwear, and enjoy your achievements as well as the way you smell of sugarcane and honey-of-rose . . . Actually, we're better at most things except producing more testosterone than we can usefully channel.'

'I can excuse everything but boredom. Boring people don't have to stay that way.'

HEDY LAMARR, ACTRESS

How to Tell if You're Boring

An unoccupied mind can become a bored mind; and bored people are deadly dull, no matter what sex they are. Often the problem is that the deadly dreary don't *see* how tedious they are to others. Ask yourself the following and find out whether you're one of life's great bores. If you're talking with friends, and decide to launch into one of your favourite stories/topics, how many of these statements apply?

◎ No one interrupts with 'Oh, that happened to me once!' or 'How funny, only the other day, I . . .' You reach the conclusion to your story without anyone else's deviations

◎ At the start of your anecdote people are sitting or standing up straight, but by the end they have relaxed into their chair, closer to horizontal than vertical, or else they stand slumped against walls and bar-tops

- ◎ Your companions pepper your story at odd intervals with short, empty phrases such as 'Oh really?' and 'How funny!'

- ◎ As you pause for breath, someone seizes the opportunity to steer you on to a whole new course, 'So, where did you go on holiday this year?'

If any or all of these statements apply to you, and if knowing that doesn't help you turn things around, perhaps the answer lies in technology. Scientists have now developed a tiny camera, small enough to be clipped surreptitiously onto your glasses and connected to a hand-held computer, which then uses face-recognition software to alert the speaker to signs of boredom or irritation in the listener. The Boredom Detector might sound a little extreme, but it could be the just the thing to save you from yourself.

'Somebody's boring me. I think it's me.'

DYLAN THOMAS, POET AND WRITER

The World's Most Boring Man

The popular online satirical news channel, thespoof.com ran a story in October 2009 of a man so dull he reduced even the reporter to sleep. Under the headline, WORLD'S MOST BORING MAN TAKES UP POST AS HUMAN ANAESTHETIC, the story told of 45-year-old Adrian Lipstick from Great Barr in Birmingham, whose reputation for boring everyone at his local pub to unconsciousness apparently reached the ears of staff at Bradford Hospital. Lipstick was allegedly offered a post boring patients into 'pre-op slumbers'. The Spoof cited a 'former friend and colleague' as having told reporters, 'He's an extremely boring, irritating twat. Mind you, so am I.'

Naturally, the story has no basis in fact; nonetheless it's compulsory reading for any crashing bores among you who still haven't got the message.

'The best way to be boring is to leave nothing out.'

VOLTAIRE, WRITER AND PHILOSOPHER

Royally Snubbed

There's nothing worse than being landed next to a proper bore at a dinner table. Trapped in an endlessly dull conversation on a subject about which you know very little and care even less. It's an experience sure to have you making a mental note to be a more generous conversationalist in future.

After a dinner engagement at which Her Royal Highness Princess Anne had discussed horses

exclusively with the person sitting to her left, her neighbour to her right felt not a little snubbed. It wasn't until coffee was served that the Princess finally turned to speak to him – and then only to ask if he would pass the sugar. Agitated by this royal lack of manners and bored to the point of mischief, the man climbed on a high horse of his own: he held out two sugar lumps placed gently on his outstretched palm and offered them to Princess Anne.

You're Only Mortal

Middle age is the time when you first face the fact that you are mortal after all. Coming to terms with this can send many of us reeling for a while, turning once more to the trappings of our former days; clutching at the illusion of eternal youth for a little while longer. But no amount of fast cars, younger women or macrobiotic diets are going to alter the fact that in the end, we're all leaving through the same door.

No Laughing Matter

A bizarre advert for a European life insurance policy has had almost 20,000 hits on the website YouTube. It shows a group of grinning adults, all smartly dressed in suits and ties, throwing a man in the air repeatedly as they merrily sing, 'For He's A Jolly Good Fellow'. As the camera pans back, we see a white-satin lined coffin surrounded by lilies and realize that the fellow in question is a stiff. The voice-over urges us all to take out this particular policy on the basis that 'your family will love you for it'. There is some talk of the ad having been banned – hardly surprising, given the flippant way it deals with death and bereavement.

But it's certainly true that in the West we are often guilty of a somewhat restrained grieving process. Actress and comedian Victoria Wood sums it up succinctly, pointing out that in India, when a man dies, his widow throws herself on the funeral pyre. Over here, says Wood, it's more like: 'Fifty ham baps, Beryl – you slice, I'll butter.'

'You can spend your whole life trying to be popular, but at the end of the day, the size of the crowd at your funeral will be largely dictated by the weather.'

FRANK SKINNER, COMEDIAN

It's Good to Have a Plan

The Scottish are known for their straight-talking attitude to life and death. The nation that advises to live life to the full on the basis that you're dead a long time, is perhaps most famously embodied in the person of much-loved comedian Billy Connolly. And this philosophy is right here in Connolly's joke: 'Two guys are talking and one says to the other, "What would you do if the end of the world was in three minutes' time?" The other one says, "I'd shag everything that moved . . . What would you do?" And he says, "I'd stand perfectly still."'

'I thought about killing myself. But I went on holiday to Belgium instead.'

STEPHEN FRY, TV PRESENTER AND ACTOR

Honouring the Dead

There are as many ways to honour your loved ones as
there are families. A well-thought out eulogy, a beautiful
headstone, or ashes scattered under a favourite rose
bush; the list is endless and highly personal. But in
2007, Rolling Stoner Keith Richards admitted to his
very own brand of memorial for his late father. 'He was
cremated and I couldn't resist grinding him up with a
bit of blow', he said. 'My dad wouldn't have cared . . . it
went down pretty well, and I'm still alive.'

> 'I'd rather be dead than singing "Satisfaction" when I'm forty-five.'
>
> MICK JAGGER, ROLLING STONE

Having the Last Laugh

Writing your last will and testament is a sombre process. But many look upon it as an opportunity to make their and lasting impression on the world. Take Iowa attorney Mr T. M. Zink, for instance, who died in 1930. In life, he was incensed that women could pursue an education beyond high school. He decided to leave a legacy that would be his parting gift to the misogynist cause. He placed $35,000 into trust for seventy-five years, long enough, he estimated, for it to have accumulated enough interest to build a substantial men-only library, a womanless learning-zone which he stipulated should carry a warning over every entrance: 'No Women Allowed'.

Thankfully Zink's daughter, Mrs Margaret Becker, to whom he had bequeathed just $5, successfully contested the will on the grounds that it constituted 'an insult to the womanhood of America, a libel and a slander against public morals'.

'When I die, I want it to be on my hundredth birthday, in my beach house on Maui, and I want my husband to be so upset he has to drop out of college.'

ROZ (PLAYED BY PERI GILPIN), IN HIT SITCOM *FRASIER*

A Final Act of Defiance

For anyone who finds fulfilment in adhering to the fine print in life, planning your death can be a golden opportunity. We all know the type: the guy who stores his socks balled up in neat pairs, meticulously sorts his recycling and files his tax returns a week early. Rob Brydon, the Welsh actor and comedian who excels at playing exactly this type, sums it up. 'I plan to put my ashes while still hot into one of those green wheelie bins. That'll show 'em.'

Don't Fear the Reaper

Death's a drag, isn't it? As if it weren't already miserable enough, the heavy mahogany of the traditional coffin, draped in lilies and lined with satin, is enough to put even the most incurable optimist on a proper downer. So why not decide now to tackle that last taboo head-on? A palliative care foundation based in Singapore staged a competition in 2010 for designers to come up with 'happy coffins'. There were more than seven hundred whimsical entries from all over the world, most of which threw a finger to traditions of sombre mourning. One entry, a French-designed coffin, resembled a crate of wine, complete with a single bottle nestling in amongst the packing straw. A label dangling from the neck of the bottle read, 'Special Vintage'. Perfect for anyone who thinks they're *premier cru*.

'I've no pretensions about immortality. I'm the same as everyone . . . just kind of lucky.'

KEITH RICHARDS, ROLLING STONE

A Fate Worse Than Death?

The great jazz musician Louis Armstrong had a love of life and a passion for what he did that was inspirational. He is also to be admired for his straight-talking attitude towards death. He once said, with that trademark twinkle in his eye, 'When I go to the Gate, I'll play a duet with Gabriel.' But after the death of his beloved personal valet Doc Pugh, when asked what had been wrong with Pugh, Louis replied philosophically, 'What was wrong with Doc? When you die, *everything* is wrong with you.'

Senior Moment Alert

For some of us age brings a welcome excuse for the idiocy we've been prone to for years. For others, 'senior moments' are an entirely new experience. It's all too easy for minor details to slip from busy minds, as former Python and legendary film-maker Terry Gilliam is happy to admit. 'I brush my teeth and then ten minutes later I go back and have to feel the toothbrush. Is it wet? Did I just brush them?'

So perhaps we should take some comfort from the fact that even the sharpest wits among us suffer from a spot of senior stupidity from time to time. And at least our senior moments don't get plastered over the World Wide Web, unlike some of these cerebrally-challenged celebrities . . .

Immortal Words

◎ 'Those who survived the San Francisco earthquake said, "Thank God, I'm still alive." But, of course, those who died, their lives will never be the same again.'
BARBARA BOXER, US SENATOR

◎ 'You guys line up alphabetically by height.'
BILL PETERSON, FLORIDA STATE FOOTBALL COACH

◎ 'I was provided with additional input that was radically different from the truth. I assisted in furthering that version.'
COL. OLIVER NORTH, EXCERPTED FROM HIS IRAN-CONTRA TESTIMONY

◎ 'What a waste it is to lose one's mind. Or not to have a mind is being very wasteful. How true that is.'
DAN QUAYLE, ACTOR

◎ 'And now the sequence of events in no particular order.'
DAN RATHER, FORMER CBS NEWS ANCHOR

◎ 'It's a great advantage to be able to hurdle with both legs.'
DAVID COLEMAN, SPORTS COMMENTATOR

◎ 'I haven't committed a crime. What I did was fail to comply with the law.'
DAVID DINKINS, NEW YORK CITY MAYOR

◎ 'We now have exactly the same situation as we had at the start of the race, only exactly the opposite.'
MURRAY WALKER, MOTORSPORTS COMMENTATOR

◎ 'We are not without accomplishment. We have managed to distribute poverty equally.'
NGUYEN CO THACH, VIETNAMESE FOREIGN MINISTER

◎ 'He dribbles a lot and the opposition don't like it – you can see it all over their faces.'
RON ATKINSON, EX-FOOTBALL MANAGER AND TV PUNDIT

◎ 'There is certainly more in the future now than back in 1964.'
ROGER DALTREY, LEAD SINGER OF THE WHO

◎ 'I never apologize. I'm sorry, but that's just the way I am.'
HOMER J. SIMPSON, FATHER OF THREE

Memorable Telly

Most of us have childhood memories of finding one or other of our parents at the top of the stairs, a bewildered look on their face, muttering to themselves, 'Now, what did I come up here for?' Sadly, we will fall victim to precisely these moments ourselves, sooner or later. American comedian John Heffron is already there. 'They always say that the older you get, you start to lose your memory', he says. 'I could be watching a TV show for forty-five minutes. Then, during commercials, I start flipping through the channels. Then I have to stop and go, "What the hell was I watching?"'

Lost: One Car, a Full Set of Marbles and a Clean Police Record

We've all been there at one time or another. After a long day or a longer night, you can find yourself staring hopelessly across a vast car park, with no clue where you parked your car. It happens; and usually the car turns up after a long and frustrating search (as you mutter obscenities under your breath).

Forty-six-year-old Craig Alberstat from Florida came up with a bizarre solution when he found himself scratching his head in a Boynton Beach parking lot in December 2010. Rather than carry on the search, he called the cops and reported it stolen. His story was an elaborate one, involving distraction by a cute girl, an assault by four thieves and, finally, grand theft auto.

Eventually, Alberstat came clean about his story and landed himself a criminal charge into the bargain.

> 'I never make stupid mistakes. Only very, very clever ones.'
>
> JOHN PEEL, RADIO BROADCASTER

Mistaken Identities

Putting names to faces can be an elusive talent as age creeps up on us. Getting someone's name wrong to their face can be embarrassing enough, but when identities are mistaken in very public forums, it can prove highly entertaining.

In July 2000, the *Observer* was forced to admit to just such a howler following its publication of a summer reading recommendation by celebrated Irish author Roddy Doyle. In fact, someone at the paper had contacted an entirely different Roddy Doyle, and an erratum was later published: 'Unfortunately, owing to a misunderstanding, the "Roddy Doyle" we spoke to, and who gave us a very interesting selection of summer reading, was a computer engineer from North London.'

A few years later, in November 2003, then British prime minister Tony Blair experienced the same phenomenon after having emailed a series of sensitive queries and memos to the Right Honourable Ronnie

Campbell, MP for Blyth Valley. The emails covered the Iraq War and the Palestinian Question, among other subjects, and included a draft of a forthcoming speech the Prime Minister intended to make, about which he had asked Ronnie for feedback.

The actual recipient, Ronnie Campbell, proprietor of the Kutting Krew hair salon in Barrow-in-Furness, was naturally very surprised, if not a little flattered, that the British prime minister should seek his opinion. Not wanting to disappoint, he replied: 'It's very good, just go ahead with it.'

'I'm not interested in age. People who tell me their age are silly. You're as old as you feel.'

ELIZABETH ARDEN, COSMETICS MAGNATE

Sex Beyond
Your Twenties

The notion that beyond your twenties you're at daily
risk of becoming sexually 'past it' is drummed into us by
an advertising industry obsessed with youth. Evidently,
by this time of life, we should all be far more interested
in golf and gardening than getting down and dirty in the
sack. But while Boy George may not be alone in
preferring a nice cup of tea to a raunchy all-nighter in
the bedroom, clearly he's in a minority.

It's well known that women don't reach their sexual
peak until their thirties (perhaps much later) and older
couples, liberated by their empty nests, can celebrate
their love as noisily as they like. So whether you fancy
embracing promiscuity with all the vigour of middle
youth or simply enjoying the lusty libido of the recently
past-it, cast aside your sudoku and drop your allotment
overalls. Haven't you heard? There *is* sex after twenty-
five!

'I think a lot about getting old. I don't want to be one of those seventy-year-olds who still wants lots of sex.'

RUPERT EVERETT, ACTOR

Whatever Turns You On . . .

Every once in a while, a story of sexual endeavour hits the news. Take, for instance, forty-something mother of three, Julie Amiri. In 1993, Julie was arrested for shoplifting on London's Oxford Street. And it wasn't her first time. In fact, she had a track record of a staggering fifty-two similar offences. What stirred Julie to steal wasn't poverty, greed or malice. For Julie, the experience of being detained by security guards and arrested by uniformed police was entirely, irresistibly intoxicating. In fact, she convinced doctors that it was the only way she could achieve orgasm, and as a result she escaped without a single conviction.

'When you've been married for a while it gets a bit boring in bed. The other day I said to my husband, "I can't remember the last time we had sex."
  He yelled back, "We're having it now!"'

VICTORIA WOOD, COMEDIAN

Sexy Straight-Talking

In these modern times, it seems that almost anything goes. You've got your eye on a woman half your age? Fine. You want an open relationship? Knock yourself out. All that matters is that you speak your mind. So when a successful divorcee in his late sixties asked his beautiful thirty-something girlfriend to marry him, he was delighted that she accepted. Still cautious, however, he insisted on a prenuptial agreement but agreed happily to most of her requests.

Her house would remain her house, she insisted. 'Naturally', he said. The convertible he bought her last birthday – she wouldn't have to give it up should the marriage come to an end? 'Absolutely not,' he assured her. As for their sex life, her interests would need protecting in this department too. She wanted to be sure her needs would be met – at least six times a week. 'No problem,' he replied, affably. 'Book me in for Saturdays.'

'As you grow older you lose interest in sex, your friends drift away and your children often ignore you. There are other advantages, of course, but these are the outstanding ones.'

RICHARD NEEDHAM, BRITISH POLITICIAN

A Red-Hot Trip Down Memory Lane

The older we get, the more distance we can put between ourselves and those early sexual exploits that can still make us cringe. Thankfully they are scenes that will replay only in the minds of the two participants . . . unless of course, there was an audience.

Pity, then, that doyenne of stage and screen Dame Judi Dench, who made a little-known film in her midforties in which she cavorted naked around an Irish country estate with a very young Jeremy Irons, and later lured him into bed with her by smearing her breasts with meringue. The sex scenes left little to the imagination, and while she had no qualms about taking on the role at the time, evidently with hindsight it is a career moment tinged with a regretful blush.

The film aired once on BBC2 in the seventies, but Dame Judi was spared the embarrassment of further

---

'One of the consequences of growing older, I find, is that you become progressively less interested in other people's sex lives. These days, frankly, I find it difficult to show much interest even in my own.'

MARTIN KELNER, WRITING IN *THE GUARDIAN*

---

screenings after the tapes lay forgotten in dusty storage at the Beeb . . . Imagine her chagrin, then, when the movie's ageing producer succeeded in getting the film released to him in 2003, and staged an exclusive viewing to the world's press gathered in New York. Critics hailed it as a 'buried treasure' . . . but not buried quite deep enough for Dame Judi's liking.

'My wife left. The first thing I noticed after she left, my clothes quit washing, and they quit drying and hanging themselves up. I figure they're depressed.'

PAT DIXON, COMEDIAN

For as Long as We Both Shall Live?

Marriage can be a messy business. For couples who let the compromises, the sacrifices and the disagreements get in their way, a midlife crisis of the marital kind can soon threaten and all too often, it can land them both in the divorce court. And we all know how that ends: formerly rational, intelligent individuals are reduced to playground bullies once they are caught in the snare of divorce. He refuses to give her the convertible; she cuts the legs off all his suits. He refuses her a £125 million settlement; she throws a jug of water over his divorce lawyer. It's an uncomfortable ending and one to be avoided.

If these horror stories don't send you scurrying back home to the wife with a bunch of freesias and a bottle of Lambrusco, there's no hope for you . . .

> 'I got off lightly. Think what I'd have had to pay Alyce if she had contributed anything to the relationship.'
>
> JOHN CLEESE, ON HIS £12 MILLION DIVORCE SETTLEMENT.

Splitting Your Assets

It's always nice to read about that rare breed of lawsuit, the amicable divorce, where the couple readily agree terms and split their assets fifty-fifty, fair and square. When 42-year-old Moeun Sarim from rural Cambodia suspected his wife of having an affair with a local police officer, he demanded a divorce. The settlement included the agreement that Sarim would take half the marital home – literally. In the presence of legal witnesses, Sarim and various family members arrived with saws and proceeded to remove precisely half the house, taking the debris away to his parents' home nearby. His wife, who denied having had an affair at all, nonetheless gave in to her ex-husband's demands, describing the settlement as 'very strange'. Anything for a quiet life.

Tough Love

Is divorce too easy these days? Those who've been through it would probably disagree, but there are plenty out there who will argue that couples need to try harder to make their marriages work instead of running straight to the lawyer's office at the first sign of trouble. US comedian Wanda Sykes has come under exactly this pressure, explaining how her mother reacted to the news that she was getting divorced. 'Let me tell you something – your father and I had a shoot-out, OK? He took one in the arm – Harry, show her where I shot you – now, see, that's love right there. You gotta learn how to work these things out. He was wrong, I shot him – you move on.'

'I thought when I was forty-one I would be married with kids. Well, to be honest, I thought I'd be divorced with weekend access.'

SEAN HUGHES, COMEDIAN

Stranger Than Fiction

By middle age, an unchecked addiction to gaming ought to be a thing of the past. You're a grown-up now: time to get a little perspective on your life. If you're not careful, all those hours devoted to your cyber-life can impact on your real-time relationships. Worse still, what happens when your addiction is so consuming, that you no longer have any real-time relationships?

In 2008, *The Times* reported on a very modern crime of passion. A respectable 43-year-old piano teacher from the southern Japanese island of Kyushu had been abandoned by the husband she loved, and in a fit of pique had been driven to commit murder. An age-old tragedy. Except that in this case the marriage had been a 'virtual' one, as had the divorce and the subsequent murder, all carried out through the highly addictive world of online fantasy game Maple Life. After her avatar had been suddenly and unceremoniously 'divorced', the piano teacher saw red. She hacked into her ex's account and systematically destroyed his avatar. Cyber-murder.

When a 33-year-old office worker from Sapporo in northern Japan discovered the 'murder' of his online persona, he was so devastated, he contacted the police.

This cyber-homicide was taken very seriously and the woman faced criminal charges and a five-year prison sentence.

'I'm going to marry a girl that's kind of cute now but is guaranteed to either gain a lot of weight or lose her looks very quickly. This way, when I trade her in for a much hotter girlfriend, my ex-wife will look even worse.'

GEOFF WOLINETZ, JOURNALIST

Till Death Us Do Part?

Divorce can be a costly business and some guys will go to any lengths to get out of paying alimony. In 2008 a Connecticut couple stood in the divorce courts after twenty-six years of marriage. Karen Finnegan cited irreconcilable differences in her suit against her husband Joseph.

But Joe wasn't prepared to pay up without a fight. He claimed that she couldn't file for divorce because a heart failure – a temporary death – some years previously was enough to dissolve his marriage. He filed a motion captioned 'Motion to Dismiss on the Grounds that the Defendant is No Longer Married to the Plaintiff Having Been Previously Completely, Although Not Permanently Dead'.

The motion was denied, on the basis that Joe's 'death' did not match up to the necessary legal definition of 'permanent' and 'irreversible cessation' of life. Nice try, Joe.

The Perils of a Visit to the Mother-in-Law

Often an infidelity doesn't remain secret for long. Hushed phone calls, later and later nights 'at the office' and unfamiliar scents lingering on suit jackets conspire to give the game away sooner or later. But in 2001, an adulterous affair was brought to the attention of a wronged wife from a bizarre source.

The wife in question returned home after a month-long spell visiting her parents. She was soon plagued by nagging doubts, triggered by the family's pet mynah bird's unusual new lexicon. Whenever the phone rang the bird became particularly vocal, twittering, 'I love you', 'Be patient', and, worse still, the word 'divorce'. The woman, convinced that the bird was testifying to her husband's infidelity, took herself and her bird to see a lawyer to start divorce proceedings.

> 'Marriage is forever. It's like cement.'
>
> PETER O'TOOLE, ACTOR

Staying Married . . . For Now

In these days of grim divorce statistics, lots of married couples going through troubled times turn to self-help manuals for inspiration. Everyone wants to beat the odds. In 1997, Patricia Allen and Sandra Harmon wrote a book entitled *Staying Married and Loving It*, packed

full of the authors' combined wisdom on the subject of long and happy marriages. The following year, the following statistics appeared in *Harper's Magazine*:

- ◎ Total number of marriages experienced by the co-authors of *Staying Married and Loving It* : 5

- ◎ Number of months one co-author spent married to the original Bozo the Clown: 18

'You have to come up with this shit every year. Last week I just wrote, "I still love you, see last year's card for full details."'

MICHAEL MCINTYRE, COMEDIAN, ON VALENTINE'S DAY CARDS

A Not-So-Spiritual Break-Up

Custody battles can be the most devastating part of divorce, but not all battles are fought over the children. When Hollywood couple Meg Ryan and Dennis Quaid separated in 2000, citing irreconcilable differences, their struggle for custody was not fought over their son Jack, then only eight years old, but over something far more bizarre. The *LA Times* reported in August 2000 that the couple were filing for exclusive custody rights over their guru and spiritual leader, Gurumayi Chidvilasananda. Both were reported as having been described by a close friend as 'guru-dependent', but the court refused to rule on access to professional services and Ryan and Quaid were left to seek enlightenment somewhere else.

In the Dog House

Every marriage has its ups and downs and at some point in the relationship, one of you is bound to end up sleeping on the couch. But 48-year-old Vlad Popescu from Romania pushed his wife Maria to the edge of endurance with his heavy drinking and indolent ways. He was so slovenly, Maria complained to the press, that the closest he'd got to doing any work in ten years was to build a dog kennel. So she booted him out of the house and into the dog kennel. Vlad complained of sub-zero temperatures but Maria was reportedly unmoved, saying, 'His boozing has made our family's life a misery until now and it's about time he woke up and experienced some of the consequences.'

> 'A good marriage would be between a blind wife and a
> deaf husband.'
>
> MICHEL DE MONTAIGNE, ESSAYIST AND STATESMAN

Battle of the Sexes

If there's one thing you should have learned by now, it's
that the battle of the sexes never really ends. Whether
it's fought over who comes out on top in the boardroom
or the bedroom, the parameters of the battleground
may change with passing years, but the fight goes on.
The only way through it is to look for the funny side.

What He Says:

◎ 'Men are far more romantic about women. Men are
the ones who'll say, "I've found somebody, She's
amazing. If I don't get to be with this person, I can't
carry on. If I'm not with her I'll end up in a bedsit,
I'll be an alcoholic." That's how women feel about
shoes.'
DYLAN MORAN, COMEDIAN

◎ 'I've got no problem buying tampons. I'm a modern
man. But apparently, they're not a "proper present".'
JIMMY CARR, COMEDIAN

◎ 'Men don't know much about women. We do know when they're happy. We know when they're crying, and we know when they're pissed off. We just don't know in what order these are going to come at us.'
EVAN DAVIES, JOURNALIST

What She Says:

◎ 'Why did God create men? Because vibrators can't mow the lawn.'
MADONNA, POP STAR

◎ 'Women speak because they wish to speak, whereas a man speaks only when driven to speech by something outside himself – like, for instance, he can't find any clean socks.'
JEAN KERR, WRITER

◎ 'To attract men, I wear a perfume called New Car Interior.'
RITA RUDNER, WRITER AND ACTRESS

When One Door Closes, Another Opens

Let's face it; statistics on marriage and divorce are hardly encouraging. Almost 50 per cent of all marriages, we are told, now end in divorce. Most of us need only take a look at our midlife friends to see these grim statistics borne out: sadly, few marriages last the course. And picking yourself up again after a nasty separation can be tough; toughest of all can be the decision about what to do with the many trinkets, souvenirs and keepsakes accrued over the course of a long relationship.

Croatian artists Olinka Vistica and Drazen Grubisic came up with an ingenious solution to this dilemma after their own relationship came to an end. They began collecting friends' and relations' mementos of lovers past. Before long, the collection filled a trailer and the travelling Museum of Broken Relationships was born.

Some of their most prized artefacts include the axe used by a woman to destroy her same-sex partner's furniture after their relationship ended badly. Under the axe, a note from the contributor reads, 'The more her room filled up with chopped-up furniture, the more I started to feel better.'

Give Yourself
a Break

For those with more free time and some spare cash, it's probably time to think about taking a holiday. But don't let anyone lure you onto a cruise ship just yet. There's still plenty of time to dream bigger than just an all-you-can-eat supper at the captain's table.

'My experience of ships is that on them one makes an interesting discovery about the world. One finds one can do without it completely.'

MALCOLM BRADBURY, NOVELIST

3.00 bingo, 4.00 tea dance, 4.30 burial at sea

Empty Nest

US comedian Jeff Allen knows exactly what it is to live your married life without a moment's peace. The demands of a busy family can mean that years go by without the two of you having a chance to get away together. So Jeff was delighted when, for the first time in more than ten years, he and his wife booked a child-free trip to Hawaii.

137

'So you parents know, after ten years, by the second day in Hawaii, we had no idea how to entertain ourselves. By the third day, we went to the beach and did what came naturally to us. We started yelling at other people's kids.'

'Don't just rule out going on a cruise. Think about it, then rule it out.'

JENNY ECLAIR, WRITER AND COMEDIAN

Travelling Light

If you think the worst part of travelling is packing your luggage perhaps you could join the growing numbers of people who are tempted to take a 'nakation' at a nudist resort. So long as you remember to slap the sun block on the parts where the sun doesn't normally shine, all should be well.

At least, that was US comedian Carol Leifer's hope. She confessed: 'Thought it would be all sexy and hot. Oh my God, what a flubber-fest! Everybody who shouldn't be naked is naked – didn't make me want to take off my clothes, made me want to take out my contacts.'

'Good morning all. I am still in Florida where it is hot and lovely. And sticky, which isn't so great at my age. Too many creases to wipe dry.'

JONATHAN ROSS, CHAT SHOW HOST, TWEETING FROM THE US

Hot Air

Do you find air travel intolerable? You're in good company . . .

◎ 'I always sit in the tail end of a plane, always, cos you never hear of a plane backing into a mountain.'
TOMMY COOPER, COMEDIAN

◎ 'If God had intended us to fly, he wouldn't have invented Spanish air traffic control.'
CRAIG CHARLES, ACTOR AND COMEDIAN

◎ 'The Devil himself had probably redesigned hell in the light of information he had gained from observing airport layouts.'
ANTHONY PRICE, NOVELIST

◎ 'Countries are actually closer than you think . . . Pilots just fly aeroplanes around longer to make you think they're far away.'
BILL BAILEY, ACTOR AND COMEDIAN

◎ 'There are two kinds of travel: first class and with children.'
JULIAN BARNES, NOVELIST

◎ 'If forced to travel on an aeroplane, try to get in the cabin with the captain, so you can keep an eye on him and nudge him if he falls asleep or point out any mountains looming up ahead.'
MIKE HARDING, COMEDIAN

'There is nothing more grotesque to me than a vacation.'
DUSTIN HOFFMAN, ACTOR

You could always try to liven up the flight . . .

◎ 'It's strange isn't it? You stand in the middle of a
library and go, "Aaaaagghhhh," and everyone just
stares at you. But you do the same thing on an
aeroplane and everyone joins in.'
TOMMY COOPER, COMEDIAN

◎ 'With the casino and the beds, our passengers will
have at least two ways to get lucky on one of our
flights.'
RICHARD BRANSON, OWNER OF VIRGIN AIRWAYS

'For a while we pondered whether to take a vacation or
get a divorce. We decided that a trip to Bermuda is over
in two weeks, but a divorce is something you always have.'

WOODY ALLEN, FILM DIRECTOR

The Terrible Tourist

Over the years tourists have earned themselves a bad reputation. The rudeness, drunkenness or arrogance of the few can land the rest of us with a label that's hard to shake. Take for instance, the English cricketer Phil Tufnell who accompanied his team to a cricket tour of India in 1993 and was reported as having said, 'I've done the elephant. I've done the poverty. I might as well go home.'

'I wouldn't mind seeing China if I could come back the same day.'

PHILIP LARKIN, POET

Ill-Fated Adventurers

You've packed the kids off so that it's just the two of you. You checked out the hotel reviews, did your research, chose the best time of year to travel; in fact, you've done everything right. And yet circumstances way beyond your control not only conspire to wreck your vacation but send governments into crisis management.

Take, for example, the middle-aged Swiss couple drawn to the stunning azure skies and turquoise ocean of the Maldives; the perfect site to renew their wedding vows after a long and happy marriage. But the ceremony resulted in a political furore after a video of the ceremony was posted on YouTube. The celebrant, addressing the couple in the local language, chanted what sounded like a prayer and a blessing; in fact, his homage to the happy couple transpired to be a torrent of abuse, accusing them of fornication and bestiality, packed with lewd sexual references and heaping insults on the couple's children.

The video went viral, the celebrants were duly arrested and the Maldives government went into diplomatic overdrive. But the lesson for all romantics out there looking to renew their vows in exotic locations – make sure you know exactly what you're saying 'I do' to!

'How on earth did Gandhi manage to walk so far in flip-flops? I can't last ten minutes in mine.'

MRS MERTON, AKA CAROLINE AHERNE, COMEDIAN AND ACTRESS

Not Well-Travelled

In 1969 portrait photographer Yousuf Karsh had a shoot with the crew of the Apollo II moon landings. Karsh photographed Neil Armstrong, Edwin Aldrin and Michael Collins, producing an iconic black-and-white image of all three men in profile. After the shoot, the men and their wives had dinner. Armstrong was fascinated to hear tales of the Karshs' travels all over the globe, but after a while Mrs Karsh grew restless. Naturally, she was far more interested in hearing about Armstrong's travels.

Armstrong was crestfallen, and told her, 'But that's the only place I've ever been.'

Just the
Two of Us

When the kids finally leave home we all react differently. Some cling to their precious offspring, sobbing wet tears into their shoulder, wailing that life will never be the same again. Others have already picked out the new office suite and fabric swatches for their vacated room before the bags are even packed. Either way, 'empty nest syndrome' involves a major overhaul of the way of life you've settled into for the past couple of decades. More to the point, once the last of your kids leave home, there's *no one to blame stuff on anymore*.

'You lose a child, you gain a sex life.'

LETTY COTTIN POGREBIN, FOUNDER OF *MS.* MAGAZINE

Letting Go of the Controls

Newspaper columnist Erma Bombeck's quirky take on family life kept many American parents going through the dark years of their offspring's adolescence. She had plenty to say about empty nest syndrome too, pointing out that what parents find so hard about the transition is not, 'mourning the passing of all those wet towels on the floor, or the music that numbs your teeth, or even the bottle of capless shampoo dribbling down the shower drain'. The problem is something much more fundamental. 'They're upset because they've gone from supervisor of a child's life to a spectator. It's like being the vice president of the United States.'

'Human beings are the only creatures on earth that allow their children to come back home.'

BILL COSBY, ACTOR AND COMEDIAN

Still the Woman I Fell in Love With . . . I Think

After their youngest child finally moved out of the house for college, a middle-aged couple dried their tears, enjoyed a candlelit supper and shared a bottle of wine in front of the fire. After reminiscing about the happy times shared when their family was young, the woman leaned over to her husband, ran her fingers through his hair and gently took off his glasses.

'You should consider laser eye surgery, honey,' she said softly. 'Without your glasses, you look almost the same as you did the day we married.'

Her husband chuckled quietly to himself. 'It's funny,' he said, 'but without my glasses on, you don't look so bad yourself.'

'Most children threaten at times to run away from home. This is the only thing that keeps some parents going.'

PHYLLIS DILLER, ACTRESS AND COMEDIAN

A Fine Romance

Lots of couples have a tough time readjusting to the new parameters of their relationship once the kids leave home. Without the noise of a houseful of teenagers to fill their down-time, it can take a while to settle into this new phase of their relationship.

When one couple in their fifties struggled to adjust to their newly empty nest, the wife came up with an idea she thought might help them make the transition.

'I think we should start dating again', she told her husband one Saturday afternoon. 'I think it would do us good: rejuvenate us both.'

Her husband agreed enthusiastically.

'Great,' his wife replied. 'So where are you taking me tonight then?'

The smile faded from her husband's face. 'You mean we're supposed to date each other?'

'I'd marry again if I found a man who had fifteen million dollars, would sign over half to me, and guarantee that he'd be dead within a year.'

BETTE DAVIS, ACTRESS

The Youth of Today

For anyone still very much in the throes of a household dominated by its adolescent inhabitants, an empty nest may seem little more than wishful thinking. Let's face it, life with teenagers can be challenging. During the six years it takes them to get from being twelve to eighteen, you age roughly twenty years. They ignore most of what you say and scoff at the rest. After all, you know nothing, you don't understand and it really isn't fair.

If it's any consolation, things have always been this way. For as long as man has been able to make written complaint, the insolence of youth has been bemoaned and bewailed by some of the greatest thinkers in history.

◎ In the fifth century BC Socrates complained: 'The children love luxury. They have bad manners, contempt for authority, show disrespect for elders, and love to chatter in place of exercise.'

◎ In the fourth century BC, Plato grumbled: 'Our youth have an insatiable desire for wealth; they have bad manners and atrocious customs regarding dressing and their hair and what garments or shoes they wear.'

◎   A thirteenth-century priest known as Peter the
    Hermit was similarly irked: 'The young people of
    today think of nothing but themselves. They have
    no reverence for their parents or old age. They are
    impatient of all restraint; they talk as if they alone
    know everything and what passes for wisdom with
    us is foolishness with them. As for the girls, they
    are foolish and immodest and unwomanly in
    speech, behaviour and dress.'

◎ And Mark Twain was man enough to admit to his own intolerable teenaged years in an article he wrote for the *Atlantic Monthly*, in 1874: 'When I was a boy of fourteen, my father was so ignorant I could hardly stand to have the old man around. But when I got to be twenty-one, I was astonished at how much he had learned in seven years.'

So, take a deep breath, keep your drinks cabinet locked and be patient: the end is nigh. And in the meantime, take some comfort from a British study carried out in 2009 that concluded that eventually we all come to appreciate everything our parents did for us. At what magic age will this happen? Apparently, you just have to keep strong until they turn twenty-two.

'One child punishes you by leaving, the other punishes us all by staying.'

PATSY (PLAYED BY JOANNA LUMLEY),
IN SITCOM *ABSOLUTELY FABULOUS*

Pioneers of
Past It

You spent your youth fearlessly speaking out against injustice wherever you found it. You partied, 'tuned out' and dropped in. Twenty years on and you're still that same strong-minded pleasure seeker, only now, your generation, with its unquenchable young-at-heart spirit, is running the world. So why should you buy into the media-myth of a sedate old age? Take heart from these pioneers who are proving that being 'past it' is merely a choice made by the uninspired, not a biological inevitability.

'If you want the God's honest truth, baby boomers are the most obnoxious people in the history of the human race.'

JOE QUEENAN, CRITIC AND WRITER

How to Be Slightly Less Well-Behaved

If you spent your twenties and thirties in a haze of terry-towelling nappies and ridiculously tiny mortgage payments, there's a good chance you've long since forgotten how to be wild. I'm guessing the closest thing you've come to breaking a rule lately has been to lash out against the one-way system round IKEA, right? If that's the case, settling down into badly behaved late middle age may prove harder than it sounds. If you worked hard to be the model spouse/parent/employee for a couple of decades, asserting your right to behave outrageously is going to take time and practice.

Why not start small? Try this six-step guide to relocating your *va va voom*:

◎ If your love life's becoming humdrum, forget the handcuffs and the feather duster: if something's worth doing, it's worth spraining a muscle for: study and practise the Kama Sutra.

◎ Take a trip somewhere warm, find a lovely moonlit ocean or starlit lake, throw aside your Speedos and go skinny-dipping.

◎ If you've never been one to work a crowd, it's high time you learned how. Go see your favourite rock band live, leave your worries about dad-dancing at the door, climb up onto the stage and throw yourself at the mercy of the crowd. Literally. Crowd surfing is uplifting stuff!

◎ If you've always been a bit of a shrinking violet, happier in the audience of life than in the spotlight, it's time to redress the balance. Put yourself up as an extra in a movie and lose yourself in the action for a while.

◎ Has it been a very long time since you've clung on to a beautiful stranger as if your life depended on it? Fear not! Sign yourself up for a charity skydive. You get to raise money for a worthy cause and see the world from a whole new perspective. All that and you get to strap yourself to the groin of a burly stranger.

'I don't need plastic surgery. I need Lourdes.'

PAUL O'GRADY, CHAT-SHOW HOST

Verdict: Rock Paper Scissors

One of the benefits of having been around the block a few times is that you've learned enough to know how to shame the new kids whenever it's called for.

In 2006 a US hotel investment firm sued an insurance company for failure to pay up on an insurance claim for damage caused by Hurricane Charley. The case would have been unremarkable had it not been for the fact that attorneys for both parties bickered like schoolboys about even the simplest of issues. When they started throwing their toys out of the pram about the location for the deposition, venerable US district judge Gregory A. Presnell could bear it no longer. With razor-sharp wit, he came up with a quirky ruling that shunned conventional dispute resolution and made legal history.

His ruling read: 'At 4.00 p.m. on Friday June 30, 2006, counsel shall convene at a neutral site agreeable to both parties. If counsel cannot agree on a neutral site, they shall meet on the front steps of the [Courthouse]. Each lawyer shall be entitled to be accompanied by one paralegal who shall act as an attendant and witness. At that time and location, counsel shall engage in one (1) game of "rock, paper, scissors". The winner of this engagement shall be entitled to select the location for the 30(b)(6) deposition to be held somewhere in Hillsborough County during the period July 11–12, 2006.'

The shamefaced attorneys settled their dispute before the Judge had a chance to resort to the naughty step.

'I refuse to admit that I am more than fifty-two, even if that makes my children illegitimate.'

NANCY ASTOR, FIRST FEMALE MP

Never Too Old to Learn New Tricks

For anyone still talking themselves into believing that their wild days are a thing of the past, take a leaf out of Dame Helen Mirren's book. At sixty-four Dame Helen scoffed at those who asked whether her naked publicity shots for her latest movie might have been ill-advised.

After all, a journalist suggested, some might have found the pictures upsetting. 'Too bad!' Dame Helen responded, rightly proud of the photos.

The movie in question was *Love Ranch* in which she plays the madam of a whorehouse, a role she says she relished. 'It's amazing how quickly you get into dildos everywhere and pink-feather handcuffs. Within an hour you're completely used to it,' she said. Once an Essex girl, always an Essex girl.

'I have enjoyed greatly the second blooming . . . suddenly you find – at the age of fifty, say – that a whole new life has opened before you.'

AGATHA CHRISTIE, NOVELIST

BIBLIOGRAPHY

Books

Powell, Michael (ed.), *The Mammoth Book of Great British Humour*, Constable & Robinson Books, London 2010

Fadiman, Clifton and Bernard, Andre, *Bartlett's Book of Anecdotes*, Little, Brown and Company, London 2000

Bussard, Paul C. and Geer, Charles (ed.), *New Catholic Treasury of Wit and Humor*, Meredith Press, New York 1968

Pilkington, Karl, *Karlology*, Dorling Kindersley, 2008

Sherrin, Ned (ed.), *The Oxford Dictionary of Humorous Quotations*, Oxford University Press, Oxford 1995

Stabiner, Karen (ed.), *The Empty Nest: 31 Parents Tell the Truth About Relationships, Love and Freedom After the Kids Fly the Coop*, Voice, 2007

Newspapers, Magazines and Periodicals

Baltimore City Paper

Daily Mail

The Daily Telegraph

Financial Times

The Guardian

The Independent

LA Times

Metro

New Statesmen

New York Daily News

The New York Times

San Francisco Chronicle

Spectator

The Times

Useful Websites

anecdotage.com

askmen.com

bbc.co.uk

brainyquote.co

comedycentral.com

dumbcriminals.com

imdb.com

msn.com

nbc.com

saidwhat.com

slate.com

spiked-online.com